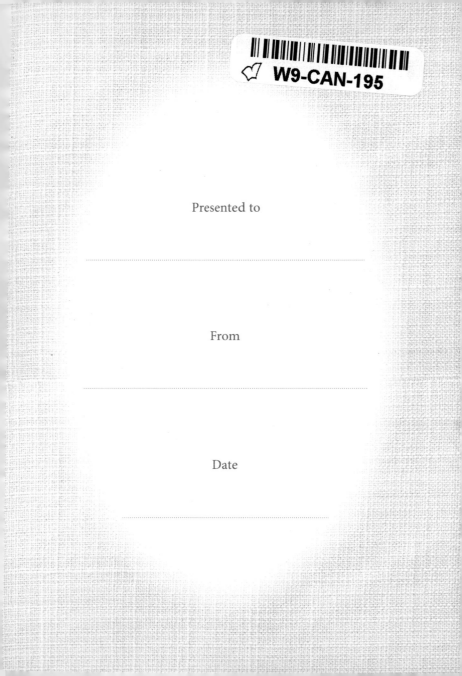

Presented to

....

From

....

Date

....

GOD'S BLESSINGS
Just for You

100 DEVOTIONS

JACK COUNTRYMAN

An Imprint of Thomas Nelson Publishers

THOMAS NELSON
Since 1798

Published in Nashville, Tennessee, by Thomas Nelson. Thomas Nelson is a registered trademark of HarperCollins Christian Publishing, Inc.

Thomas Nelson titles may be purchased in bulk for educational, business, fund-raising, or sales promotional use. For information, please email SpecialMarkets@ThomasNelson.com.

Scripture quotations are taken from the New King James Version®. © 1982 by Thomas Nelson. Used by permission. All rights reserved.

Any Internet addresses, phone numbers, or company or product information printed in this book are offered as a resource and are not intended in any way to be or to imply an endorsement by Thomas Nelson, nor does Thomas Nelson vouch for the existence, content, or services of these sites, phone numbers, companies, or products beyond the life of this book.

ISBN 978–1–4002–1818–9
ISBN 978–1–4002–1861–5 (ebook)

Printed in India

20 21 22 23 24 BPI 10 9 8 7 6 5 4 3 2 1

Contents

INTRODUCTION

*T*he Bible often speaks of the blessings God has for us when we walk in His way. Following His simple-to-understand—but not always easy-to-live-out—guidelines for our attitudes and behavior can definitely mean experiencing life's most wonderful blessings.

Yet some of these blessings come unexpectedly. As Christians, we want to be sensitive to God's often quiet, gentle leadings so we don't miss a single blessing He has for us. Has God recently been asking you—nudging you—to do something you've not yet done? Perhaps He has had you thinking about reading His Word more regularly? I hope so.

This book highlights one hundred passages of Scripture that will enrich your walk with God and encourage you to obey His commands. As you ponder the blessings implicit in these instructions, you will see more clearly that God desires to have a close, personal relationship with you and, along the way, to bless you in ways far greater than you can ask or imagine.

I encourage you to walk hand in hand with God every single day. You'll be amazed by His blessings!

The Lord has been mindful of us;
He will bless us. . . .
He will bless those who fear the Lord,
Both small and great. . . .
May you be blessed by the Lord,
Who made heaven and earth.

PSALM 115:12–13, 15

1

"Who? Me?"

Look at the blessing revealed in the first line of today's scripture: God Himself—the Creator and Sustainer of all that exists, the Author of history—"has been mindful of us"! Yes, you—and me! He knows who we are. He is aware of our needs and concerns, our dreams and desires. What a blessing!

And God wants to bless us more as we honor Him with our life. In fact, the closer we walk with Jesus, the more like Him we will become. Then, when God uses us to bless someone else, that person may see Jesus reflected in us.

When we place other people's needs and desires before our own, we are in a position to be a blessing. In fact, we are living in a way that glorifies God when we ask Him to use us to bless someone. And what a joy and a blessing to know that God uses us to bless others.

May we live thanking God for all His blessings and yielded to His using us to bless others!

"Blessed are those servants whom the master, when he comes, will find watching. Assuredly, I say to you that he will gird himself and have them sit down to eat, and will come and serve them. And if he should come in the second watch, or come in the third watch, and find them so, blessed are those servants. . . . Blessed is that servant whom his master will find [watching for him] when he comes."

JESUS IN LUKE 12:37–38, 43

2

SERVING AS JESUS SERVED

*B*e prepared" is the classic Boy Scout motto. It is also God's serious call to us, His people: Are we prepared for—and are we watching for—the second coming of Jesus?

No one knows when He, the sacrificial Lamb of God, will return to this earth as the victorious, reigning Lion of God. But we who love Jesus are not to wait idly for that moment. We are to stay busy serving, worshiping, evangelizing, and investing in our relationship with our Lord.

As Jesus taught in today's passage, when He returns and finds us ready to welcome Him, He will "have [us] sit down to eat, and will come and serve [us]." What an amazing reward for our obedience!

And what a blessed obedience it is when we serve people the way Jesus served. When we give ourselves away as our Savior gave Himself away, our service on His behalf is actually a form of worship.

What a blessing to have a purpose in life, a God to serve, and a Savior to love!

Bless the LORD, *O my soul;*
And all that is within me,
  bless His holy name!
Bless the LORD, *O my soul,*
And forget not all His benefits:
Who forgives all your iniquities,
Who heals all your diseases,
Who redeems your life from destruction,
Who crowns you with lovingkindness
  and tender mercies,
Who satisfies your mouth with good things,
So that your youth is renewed
  like the eagle's.

PSALM 103:1–5

3

BLESSED BENEFITS

*L*ook at today's passage and the truths the psalmist set forth. Starting with the fifth line, read each line slowly. Imagine you're hearing those remarkable words for the first time. Then consider times in your life when our faithful God has blessed you in each of those ways:

- What sin did He forgive—and enable you to forgive yourself for?
- When have you experienced God's healing?
- What redemptive act of bringing beauty from ashes has the Lord done in your life?
- What specifics come to mind when you think of God's loving-kindness to you? When you think of His tender mercies?
- With what good things does God satisfy your mouth?
- When have you experienced Him renewing your energy?

As you thank God for these promises kept and blessings received, be encouraged that He will always keep His promises.

[Thomas] said to [his fellow disciples],
"Unless I see in [Jesus'] hands the print
of the nails, and put my finger into the
print of the nails, and put my hand
into His side, I will not believe."

And after eight days [Jesus'] disciples were
again inside, and Thomas with them.
Jesus came, the doors being shut, and stood
in the midst, and said, "Peace to you!"

JOHN 20:25-26

4

DOUBT . . . REDEEMED

Have you ever met a fellow believer who has never wrestled with doubts about his or her faith? Probably never.

Doubts arise for various reasons. In Thomas's case, he was asked to believe the unbelievable. He doubted that Jesus had risen from the dead . . . even though Jesus had raised Lazarus and even though Jesus had told His disciples about His death and resurrection.

Sometimes doubters simply don't want to believe the gospel because they know they will have to surrender to God's will and change how they live. We all find it hard to let God be in charge.

Finally, even the strongest believers can find themselves doubting God—His goodness, His power, His love, even His existence—when life brings pain.

Doubt, however, can serve a good purpose, compelling us to determine what we believe and why, and deepening our relationship with God as we lean into Him with our pain.

Our Redeemer is able to redeem our doubt.

I wait for the Lord, my soul waits,
And in His word I do hope.
My soul waits for the Lord
More than those who watch
for the morning—
Yes, more than those who
watch for the morning.

PSALM 130:5-6

5

WAITING . . . AND WAITING

*W*aiting. No one likes it. We don't want to wait in a long line at Costco or wait for God to send the spouse we're praying for. It's hard to wait to hear from the school we want to attend or the company we want to work for. It's tough to wait for lab results—and for labor pains to start after a long thirty-eight weeks. We don't like to wait: we want what we want, and we want it right now.

The fact is, either we are unaware or we are ignoring the fact that waiting is God's training ground for strengthening our faith. As we wait, we learn to trust God more. We may not understand the circumstances of our life or why we have to wait, but we can remind ourselves that God, our heavenly Father, is in control and that His plans for us are plans for good (Jeremiah 29:11).

Also, during a season of waiting, we can practice listening for the Lord and resting in His presence. Precious blessings can come even as we wait.

The Revelation of Jesus Christ, which God gave Him to show His servants—things which must shortly take place. And He sent and signified it by His angel to His servant John, who bore witness to the word of God, and to the testimony of Jesus Christ, to all things that he saw. Blessed is he who reads and those who hear the words of this prophecy, and keep those things which are written in it; for the time is near.

REVELATION 1:1–3

6

GOD WINS!

God gave us all sixty-six books of the Bible for doctrine, reproof, correction, instruction in righteousness, and equipping for every good work (2 Timothy 3:16–17). But He promised a special blessing to those of us who read the book of Revelation and who "hear the words of this prophecy."

God gave Jesus the revelation, and Jesus shared it with His servant-angels. Then Jesus chose one of His angels to share the revelation with the apostle John, who, through his writings, would share this truth with all believers, his contemporaries, and all of God's people from that day forward.

The time for the fulfillment of Revelation prophecy is near—and nearer today than when John recorded for future generations his vision of the final battle between good and evil and of God's sealed and secure victory of good over evil. Even when we don't understand much about all the imagery and symbolism of Revelation, this takeaway is sufficient: God wins.

Praise the LORD!
Blessed is the man who fears the LORD,
Who delights greatly in His
commandments. . . .
A good man deals graciously and lends;
He will guide his affairs with discretion.
Surely he will never be shaken;
The righteous will be in
everlasting remembrance.

PSALM 112:1, 5-6

7

MAKING A DIFFERENCE

God wants us to fear Him, to respect and honor Him, and to be faithful followers who live according to His commands and in the center of His will. God also wants to bless other people through us, through what we say to them and how we interact with them. How can we make a difference in someone's life?

The psalmist described a person who is gracious, humble, and rock-solid in his commitment to God. That countercultural person can make a difference.

Also, our offerings at church bless people in need in the church body, in the community, and around the world.

We who have been blessed by God's love can also be a blessing by sharing His love with others. In fact, God may use our choice to love people with Jesus' sacrificial and winsome love to transform their lives.

May we live in a way that honors God, shows our friends that we belong to the Lord, and makes them want to follow Jesus too.

It shall come to pass, because you listen to these judgments, and keep and do them, that the LORD your God will keep with you the covenant and the mercy which He swore to your fathers. And He will love you and bless you and multiply you; He will also bless the fruit of your womb and the fruit of your land, your grain and your new wine and your oil, the increase of your cattle and the offspring of your flock, in the land of which He swore to your fathers to give you. You shall be blessed above all peoples; there shall not be a male or female barren among you or among your livestock.

MOSES IN DEUTERONOMY 7:12–14

8

GOD IS LOVE

I hope this next statement doesn't shock you, but God does not love you and me because we are lovable. God loves us because His very nature is love. He can't do anything *but* love. Even His wrath and judgments reveal His love for people whose self-destructive ways He longs to have them stop.

God, who is love, is also our Creator, so we are precious in His sight. God loves us through and through, and He loves us enough not to let us stay stuck in our sin. Jesus died on the cross so that we might be forgiven, be filled with His Spirit who transforms us, and have life everlasting with Him.

Every page of the Bible reveals an aspect of God's love. So whenever we open its covers, may we also open our hearts and minds to the wonderful truth of His love. May we praise God as David did:

> Bless the LORD, O my soul;
> And all that is within me, bless His holy name!
> (Psalm 103:1)

———— ·❧ • ❧· ————

O LORD, You have searched
me and known me.
You know my sitting down
and my rising up;
You understand my thought afar off.
You comprehend my path
and my lying down,
And are acquainted with all my ways.
For there is not a word on my tongue,
But behold, O LORD, You know it altogether.

PSALM 139:1–4

———— · ————

9

BEING KNOWN BY GOD

*I*n today's scripture David expressed his wonder and awe at God's perfect knowledge of every human being He has ever created. With amazement David acknowledged that there was not one thing God did not know about him—or about you and me.

Let's try to get our minds around this truth: although more than seven billion people populate this planet, God is intimately acquainted with you, with me, with each one of us. God knows our words and deeds. In fact, He knows our thoughts and motives even more clearly than we sometimes do. As our Creator, God knows us from the inside out. As our Good Shepherd, He knows when we sit down to relax and when we rise up to engage in the activities of life. He not only knows our thoughts, but He also knows what we will say before we say it.

Nothing about us is hidden from the Lord. And even though His knowledge of us is inconceivably absolute, He absolutely loves us. And He always will.

— ❦ • ❦ —

*Repent therefore and be converted, that
your sins may be blotted out, so that
times of refreshing may come from the
presence of the Lord. . . . You are sons of
the prophets, and of the covenant which
God made with our fathers, saying to
Abraham, "And in your seed all the families
of the earth shall be blessed." To you first,
God, having raised up His Servant Jesus,
sent Him to bless you, in turning away
every one of you from your iniquities.*

PETER PREACHING IN ACTS 3:19, 25–26

10

Blessed to Share the Gospel

*H*aving just seen Peter and John heal a lame man, the people of Jerusalem wanted to know more. Peter credited the miracle to the power of Jesus, whom they had demanded that Pilate crucify (Acts 3:13–15).

Jesus' death on the cross was actually the fulfillment of God's prophecies and plan. God sent His Son into the world to die for our sins so that we could know His forgiveness and enter into a relationship with our holy Lord. Furthermore, when He walked on this earth, Jesus showed us how we should live and how we should love God, one another, and even our enemies.

In his sermon Peter reminded his Jewish audience that God had greatly blessed their ancestor Abraham so that Abraham could bless others. Now the Jews were blessed with the opportunity to confess their sin and accept Jesus as the sacrifice for those sins—and they were to bless others by sharing the good news of Jesus.

Likewise, we who are blessed to know Jesus are to share that blessed knowledge with others.

In You, O Lᴏʀᴅ, I put my trust. . . .
Bow down Your ear to me,
Deliver me speedily;
Be my rock of refuge,
A fortress of defense to save me.
For You are my rock and my fortress;
Therefore, for Your name's sake,
Lead me and guide me.

PSALM 31:1–3

11

CHOOSING TO TRUST

When we name Jesus our Savior and Lord, we place our trust in Him. We surrender our lives to Him, to do His work in His way at His time and for His glory. We trust Him to protect us and guide us.

But that salvation moment is not the only time we choose to trust Jesus. We need to choose to place our trust in Him again and again and again. We choose to entrust our day to Him when we wake in the morning. We trust Him to bless our efforts at work—in an office or at home, paid or volunteer. We trust our loved ones to Him as they come and go. Again and again we entrust our lives, our very beings, to Him who is our Refuge, our Rock, and our Fortress.

We can go to Jesus at any time, whatever the circumstances, and He will listen. We can trust the Lord for anything and everything—we can trust Him with all of our hearts and souls—because of the rock-solid truth that He loves us with an everlasting love.

As [Jesus and His disciples] were eating,
Jesus took bread, blessed and broke
it, and gave it to the disciples and
said, "Take, eat; this is My body."

Then He took the cup, and gave thanks,
and gave it to them, saying, "Drink from
it, all of you. For this is My blood of the
new covenant, which is shed for many for
the remission of sins. But I say to you, I
will not drink of this fruit of the vine from
now on until that day when I drink it
new with you in My Father's kingdom."

MATTHEW 26:26–29

12

THE LORD'S SUPPER

*T*he ceremony that we call the Lord's Supper has its roots in the last meal Jesus had with His disciples before He was arrested, flogged, and crucified. As they ate, Jesus explained the significance of the bread and wine His Jewish disciples knew well, but there was a twist. Jesus presented the bread and the wine as His body and His blood.

Two millennia later Jesus' followers still eat the bread and drink the wine as a remembrance of His sacrificial death on the cross. Taking on the punishment for our sins, Jesus gave His body—broken by the nails in His hands and feet—and His blood—poured out by the lashing and the crown of thorns.

When God looks at us, He sees us cleansed of our sins because of what Jesus did for us on the cross. Whenever we partake of the Lord's Supper, a meal reflecting God's amazing grace, we are to do so with repentant hearts, thankful for the blessings of forgiveness, a relationship with God, and eternal life.

*Oh, give thanks to the L*ORD*, for He is good!*
For His mercy endures forever.

PSALM 118:29

13

OUR GOOD GOD

What specific blessings do you think of when you hear the statement "God is good"?

It is my prayer—for all of us—that we don't just think of stuff. Yes, God blesses us with tangibles: with family, friends, food, clothing, shelter, cars, paychecks . . . The list goes on and on.

But the best blessing our good God gives is the opportunity to be in relationship with Him. Thanks to His gift of Jesus, who died for our sins and thereby bridged the gap between holy God and unholy us, we can actually know God, not just know *about* Him.

And relationships are the true gifts in life. Maybe you've noticed, for instance, that the more Christmases we celebrate, the more we value and appreciate the blessings of relationships. We savor the gift of time with people we love. The actual relationship matters more than any present these dear people might bring.

May we be grateful for the many tangible blessings God gives us, but may we appreciate even more the blessing of knowing God Himself.

Blessed is the man
Who walks not in the counsel
of the ungodly,
Nor stands in the path of sinners,
Nor sits in the seat of the scornful;
But his delight is in the law of the LORD,
And in His law he meditates day and night.

PSALM 1:1–2

14

WALKING IN THE LIGHT

G od loves to bless His children! He loves to bless us with guidance and protection as well as with food, clothing, and shelter—and parents understand the joy of blessing their kids.

One way God blesses us is by using His Word to light the path for us to walk. We live in spiritual darkness when we don't know Jesus as our Savior. Emotional and psychological darkness can result from our decisions or other people's actions. The loss of our health, the end of a relationship, or the death of a loved one also brings darkness.

When we choose to follow God, though, He doesn't leave us in the dark. Instead, speaking through His Word and by the power of His Spirit within us, He who is the Light of the World guides us and protects us, and along the way He helps us become more like Jesus.

God is with us in the darkness—what a blessing!— but He wants to lead us out of it. So, acting on a promise, He blesses us by lighting the way. Will we follow?

Blessed is he who considers the poor;
The LORD will deliver him
in time of trouble.
The LORD will preserve him
and keep him alive,
And he will be blessed on the earth.

PSALM 41:1–2

15

DOING THE WORK OF CHRIST

Look at the promises God makes to the person "who considers the poor." That person will be delivered from trouble, preserved when danger strikes, kept alive when death threatens, and "blessed on the earth." These broad categories leave room for lots of blessings!

Now, considering the poor means more than just noticing them or thinking about them. Jesus-followers are to act. As John wrote, "Whoever has this world's goods, and sees his brother in need, and shuts up his heart from him, how does the love of God abide in him? . . . Let us not love in word or in tongue, but in deed and in truth" (1 John 3:17–18).

Remember the good Samaritan? Rather than just considering the half-dead man, the Samaritan bandaged the man's wounds, took him to an inn, and paid the innkeeper to care for him (Luke 10:33–35).

When we've thought about the poor, what have we done? In what ways have we loved "in deed"? Let's ask God to show us whom to serve and how to serve—and then let's serve. Doing so is, in itself, a blessing!

*[Jesus] said, "Bring [the boy's lunch]
here to Me." Then He commanded the
multitudes to sit down on the grass. And
He took the five loaves and the two fish,
and looking up to heaven, He blessed
and broke and gave the loaves to the
disciples; and the disciples gave to the
multitudes. So they all ate and were filled,
and they took up twelve baskets full of
the fragments that remained. Now those
who had eaten were about five thousand
men, besides women and children.*

MATTHEW 14:18–21

16

FIVE LOAVES AND TWO FISH

*F*ive thousand.

Adding women and children, the crowd could have been ten thousand or fifteen thousand or more! That's a lot of mouths to feed!

Not at all intimidated, Jesus asked His disciples about available resources. Andrew had learned about a boy who had "five barley loaves and two small fish" (John 6:9). As part of this boy's lunch, those loaves and fish were undoubtedly small. In light of the crowd's great need, the bread and fish must have seemed utterly insignificant to the disciples.

Yet Jesus saw the need of the people, and He met that need in an unorthodox, unexpected, even miraculous way. Jesus will meet our needs as well. His ways may be unorthodox. His timing may be unexpected. His response might even be miraculous. We can be sure, however, that He will respond—and He will do so generously. After all, when He finished feeding the crowd, the disciples filled twelve baskets with leftovers!

Create in me a clean heart, O God,
And renew a steadfast spirit within me.
Do not cast me away from Your presence,
And do not take Your Holy Spirit from me.

PSALM 51:10–11

17

FORGIVEN AND CLEANSED

We get way too comfortable with our sin. Thankfully, our holy heavenly Father can gently help us recognize how unclean our hearts really are. Unclean hearts can come between us and God, and we can easily feel "cast . . . away from [His] presence."

Today's verses suggest that King David experienced such feelings after a man of God confronted him about committing adultery with Bathsheba and having her husband murdered (2 Samuel 11). Recognizing his sin, David acknowledged to his holy God, "Against You, You only, have I sinned, and done this evil in Your sight" (Psalm 51:4). Humbled and contrite, David turned to God and asked for forgiveness and cleansing.

Sinners by nature, we praise Jesus for His sacrificial death on the cross. The sinless Lamb of God took the punishment for our sins so that we may confess those sins and know the Lord's forgiveness and cleansing. As hymn writer Fanny Crosby put it a hundred years ago, "What a wonderful Savior is Jesus my Lord, a wonderful Savior to me."

Now it shall come to pass, if you diligently obey the voice of the LORD your God, to observe carefully all His commandments which I command you today, that the LORD your God will set you high above all nations of the earth. And all these blessings shall come upon you and overtake you, because you obey the voice of the LORD your God. . . . He will bless you in the land which the LORD your God is giving you.

MOSES IN DEUTERONOMY 28:1–2, 8

18

OVERTAKEN BY BLESSINGS

Throughout Scripture—and today's passage is an example—God promises His blessings for people who choose to obey Him. It's a promise He makes: we can be assured of His blessings when we obey God's commandments.

But may we not obey simply to receive His blessings on "[our] storehouses and in all to which [we] set [our] hand[s]." May we who belong to Jesus, who live with Him as our Savior and Lord, obey God's commands because we love and want to please our heavenly Father. May knowing that we are pleasing our Lord be in itself a life-giving blessing.

Also, when we live in obedience to God—when we conduct ourselves in a way that honors the Lord—other people may see Christ in us. We must let the light of the Lord shine through every aspect of our lives so that people living in the darkness of not knowing Jesus will be drawn to His light. What a blessing to be used by God in that way! Obey and, yes, be blessed. In fact, be overtaken by blessings!

In You, O Lᴏʀᴅ, I put my trust;
Let me never be put to shame. . . .
You are my rock and my fortress.

PSALM 71:1, 3

19

What Are We Worshiping?

Old Testament prophets boldly spoke of the foolishness of taking part of a log, carving it into an image from nature, bowing down to worship it . . . and tossing the other part of that log into the fire to bake bread. Today we are much more sophisticated in our choice of false gods. Depending on our circle, we worship, for instance, money, prestige, possessions, accomplishment, education, and power.

But God alone—the true and living God—is worthy of our worship. He alone is worthy of our trust. He alone gives us purpose, His love gives us significance, and His character makes Him our Rock and our Fortress.

Our God also commands us to speak out in our culture, which knows little, if anything, about salvation. When we obey the Great Commission and talk to people about our relationship with Jesus—and obeying God is one way we worship Him—we may be blessed to witness someone choosing to trust Jesus as Savior and Lord.

May God give us the heart to tell others about Jesus and to trust Him with the results.

*Rejoice always, pray without ceasing,
in everything give thanks; for this is the
will of God in Christ Jesus for you.*

1 THESSALONIANS 5:16–18

20

THE BLESSING OF PRAYER

Let's get practical. What did the apostle Paul actually mean when he wrote, "Pray without ceasing"? Clearly he wasn't telling us to walk around all day, mumbling prayers to God. No, Paul was addressing the attitude of our hearts, about being sensitive to God's presence, open to His direction, yielded to His will, and ready to release every concern to Him. With this heart attitude, we truly are living a life of unceasing prayer even as we go about our daily routine.

Now, on some days—when we go to church, have Bible study, meet with our home group, or visit a hurting friend—we will pray more than we do on other days. But regardless of what's on the day's agenda, we can maintain an attitude of prayer that impacts our whole life. Then, rather than having to decide, *Should I pray?*, prayer is our immediate response to any challenge or difficult situation that arises. Furthermore, this heart attitude toward prayer also keeps us close to our heavenly Father.

What a blessing prayer is!

*Blessed be the L*ORD *my Rock,*
Who trains my hands for war,
And my fingers for battle—
My lovingkindness and my fortress,
My high tower and my deliverer,
My shield and the One in
whom I take refuge,
Who subdues my people under me.

PSALM 144:1–2

21

LIVING AS THOUGH YOU KNOW GOD

*I*n Psalm 144, you can see the confidence of David the warrior. He knew that God was all he needed on the battlefields where Israel fought as well as in the battles of life that he faced.

David the poet described the Lord as his Rock, his loving-kindness, his fortress, his high tower, his deliverer, his shield, his refuge, and his victory. Wow! What more could he—or you or me or anyone else—desire?

Are you living as if God is your Rock, your fortress, your shield, and your refuge? If, for instance, God truly is your Rock, that fact will be evident in how you live. Are you calm and confident as you fight the battles of your life? Are you building your life on the solid foundation of a relationship with Jesus?

And if God is your refuge, you will almost automatically turn to Him in prayer whenever the storms of life rage, someone's words pierce your heart, or you are struggling with worry or reeling in pain. Let God be all He wants to be for you.

"Blessing I will bless you, and multiplying I will multiply your descendants as the stars of the heaven and as the sand which is on the seashore; and your descendants shall possess the gate of their enemies. In your seed all the nations of the earth shall be blessed, because you have obeyed My voice."

GENESIS 22:17–18

22

God Provides

*I*n a command that foreshadowed the future sacrifice of His own Son, God told Abraham to sacrifice his long-awaited son, Isaac, as a burnt offering—and demonstrating a remarkable trust in God, Abraham set out in obedience to His command. Abraham gathered the wood he would need and headed for Mount Moriah to make the sacrifice.

What would we do if God commanded us to sacrifice a loved one? May we learn from Abraham, who chose to believe what he told Isaac: "God will provide . . . the lamb" (Genesis 22:8). And God did. When Abraham "stretched out his hand and took the knife to slay his son" (v. 10), the angel of the Lord stopped him. Abraham looked up and saw a ram in a nearby thicket. God did provide.

God loves to bless His children in many ways. By His grace, not all of those blessings are contingent on our perfect obedience. But let's choose to obey the One we call "Lord," knowing that all of His commands are for our own good.

Trust in the L<small>ORD</small>, *and do good . . .*
Delight yourself also in the L<small>ORD</small>,
And He shall give you the
desires of your heart.
Commit your way to the L<small>ORD</small>,
Trust also in Him,
And He shall bring it to pass.

PSALM 37:3–5

23

TRUSTING AND DELIGHTING IN THE LORD

God's Word is very practical. Consider, for instance, what today's passage shows us about how to walk in a way that honors Him.

First, we find the call to "trust in the LORD, and do good." Trust is basic to our living with Jesus as Lord of our life. Trusting God implies surrendering to His will and His ways, and our doing good demonstrates that surrender. Doing good—being God's hands and feet on this earth—honors Him.

Second is the call to "delight yourself . . . in the LORD"—and what an amazing promise follows. "[God] shall give you the desires of your heart" does not mean that He will give us everything we desire. That statement means instead that God will put into our hearts the desires He wants us to have so that we will walk according to His good plans for us.

When we choose to trust God and open our hearts to His plans for us, we are able to walk hand in hand with the Lord, enjoying the blessing of His presence with us.

*Blessed is the nation whose
God is the L*ORD*,
The people He has chosen as
His own inheritance.*

PSALM 33:12

24

CHOSEN BY GOD

Long ago God chose Abraham to be the father of His people, and Abraham's descendants became known as the nation of Israel. God blessed His chosen people so that they could bless others, including people outside their nation.

The greatest blessing God has sent to the non-Jewish (Gentile) world—to you and to me—through His people Israel is the Messiah Himself:

> Is [the Lord Jesus] the God of the Jews only? Is He not also the God of the Gentiles? (Romans 3:29)

God chose the Jews as His own, but He also graciously welcomes individuals who believe that Jesus died for their sins. As the apostle Peter later wrote to believers, Jew and Gentile alike, "You are a chosen generation . . . that you may proclaim the praises of Him who called you out of darkness into His marvelous light" (1 Peter 2:9).

*You are my hope, O Lord G*od;
You are my trust from my youth.
By You I have been upheld from birth. . . .
O God, You have taught me from my youth;
And to this day I declare Your
wondrous works. . . .
Your righteousness, O God, is very high,
You who have done great things;
O God, who is like You?

PSALM 71:5–6, 17, 19

25

OUR INCOMPARABLE GOD

*A*ll good gifts come from our good—and gracious and generous—God. Consider the gifts mentioned in today's scripture:

- Sovereign, wise, and all-loving, God is the source of genuine hope.
- A faithful promise keeper and unchanging in His character, God is trustworthy.
- Our Protector, Provider, Guide, and Shepherd, God has been with us since our birth.
- The all-knowing Teacher, He has instructed us since our youth.

For these reasons and many others, we praise God's glorious name and "declare [His] wondrous works."

Knowing of God's mighty power, limited only by His perfect wisdom and eternal love, brings the blessing of peace. Our awareness of God's goodness to us brings the blessing of joy. Recognizing God's gospel of grace brings the blessings of being adopted as His child and of being in an intimate relationship with our Father.

O Lord GOD, You are God, and Your words are true, and You have promised this goodness to Your servant. Now therefore, let it please You to bless the house of Your servant, that it may continue before You forever; for You, O Lord GOD, have spoken it, and with Your blessing let the house of Your servant be blessed forever.

KING DAVID IN 2 SAMUEL 7:28–29

26

PRAYING SCRIPTURE

God speaks to us through the Bible. That's why slowing down both to meditate on what we read and to pray to God the words He Himself has given us will help us know Him better and more easily recognize His voice.

Also, did you notice that David reminded God of His promised "goodness to Your servant"? David understood that by praying according to God's promises, he aligned himself with God's will. We can do the same today: we can pray God's promises back to God.

Fervently and fruitfully, David also pursued the godly endeavor of meditating on God's Word. He wrote many of the psalms we cherish today after quietly waiting on the Lord and listening for His voice until he heard it.

In our overscheduled lives, we find it difficult to slow down, read a Bible passage, and listen for what God may be saying to us. With so many responsibilities, commitments, and people clamoring for attention, who can make time for prayer and meditation? You and I can— and I hope we will.

The LORD is great and greatly to be praised;
He is to be feared above all gods.
For all the gods of the peoples are idols,
But the LORD made the heavens.
Honor and majesty are before Him;
Strength and beauty are in His sanctuary.

PSALM 96:4–6

27

Singing Praise to God

*I*t's easy for us human beings to get used to what we see all the time:

The Maui locals sit on the beach, reading the paper, while migrating whales swim by, breaching the water, slapping it with their tails, and putting on quite a show.

Year-round residents of Park City, Utah, don't gasp at the magnificent snow-covered mountains the way first-time visitors do.

And, sadly, those of us who love the Lord may also get numb to His greatness and majesty, to His beauty and strength. What can we do to prevent that in ourselves?

Music is an ideal tool for keeping our hearts in tune with the awe and worshipful attitude due our almighty God. When we sing to the Lord, we can't help but taste the joy of being God's children.

Like the psalmist, we are to praise the Lord for His greatness, honor, majesty, strength, and beauty. Let's incorporate into our daily routine a song that facilitates our praise.

"I will make a covenant of peace with [My people], and cause wild beasts to cease from the land; and they will dwell safely in the wilderness and sleep in the woods. I will make them and the places all around My hill a blessing; and I will cause showers to come down in their season; there shall be showers of blessing."

EZEKIEL 34:25–26

28

SHOWERS OF BLESSING

In Ezekiel 34, God spoke of the leaders of Israel as shepherds who had failed in their assignment. They had fed themselves rather than their flocks. They didn't strengthen the weaker sheep, heal the sick ones, or seek after the lost ones. In sharp contrast is our true Shepherd, our Good Shepherd, who carefully tends every sheep in His flock. He provides all that they—all that we—need.

Most important, our true Shepherd has provided a way for us to be in a relationship with Him. This Shepherd—our Shepherd Jesus—wants an intimate connection with those He loves. He invites us to totally depend on Him, and He promises to send showers of blessings in due season.

One more thing. Remember: the Lord does whatever He does for our benefit. Jesus feeds us what He knows will give us health. He makes us lie down when we would rather keep moving. Jesus is the Good Shepherd, and we are His flock. Praise the Lord for the showers of His blessings.

Remember me, O Lord, with the favor
You have toward Your people.
Oh, visit me with Your salvation,
That I may see the benefit
of Your chosen ones,
That I may rejoice in the
gladness of Your nation,
That I may glory with Your inheritance.

PSALM 106:4–5

29

HALLELUJAH! WHAT A SAVIOR!

When Jesus was on the cross, one of the thieves crucified with Him said, "Lord, remember me when You come into Your kingdom" (Luke 23:42).

Considering how we live, we, too, need to cry out to God. If we're honest, confessing our sins could be a full-time job for us human beings. We are surrounded by temptation, weakened by jealousy and pride, not trusting God's nature or His Word—and the list goes on.

In Old Testament times, the forgiveness of sins required the shedding of blood: "Every priest stands ministering daily and offering repeatedly the same sacrifices, which can never take away sins" (Hebrews 10:11). When Jesus, the perfect Lamb, came to earth, the situation changed. Jesus shed His blood once and for all. No more sacrifices necessary!

And when we cry out to God, we have His unshakable promise that He will bless us with forgiveness, His favor, and the glory of our heavenly inheritance.

Blessed is the man who endures temptation;
for when he has been approved, he will
receive the crown of life which the Lord
has promised to those who love Him.
Let no one say when he is tempted, "I
am tempted by God"; for God cannot
be tempted by evil, nor does He Himself
tempt anyone. But each one is tempted
when he is drawn away by his own desires
and enticed. Then, when desire has
conceived, it gives birth to sin; and sin,
when it is full-grown, brings forth death.

JAMES 1:12–15

30

GOD'S HELP WHEN
SATAN TEMPTS

*I*n this fallen world, no human being avoids temptation. In fact, Satan often seems to work overtime to draw us away from the Lord and to entice us into activities that would undermine our Christian faith. We need to resist the devil. We are to overcome temptation when it arises. When we turn to God for His help and we stand strong, we will be blessed. That's the opening promise of today's passage.

The passage goes on to teach that whatever temptations we face in life, we must never blame God. He has promised that He will never tempt us, and we can trust Him to keep that promise.

Finally, we are to flee from our own selfish desires and rely on God to help us live in a way that glorifies His holy name. Longing for that to happen, God—by His Spirit—enables us to stand strong against the evil one and then blesses us abundantly.

I will praise You with my whole heart;
Before the gods I will sing praises to You.
I will worship toward Your holy temple,
And praise Your name
For Your lovingkindness and Your truth.

PSALM 138:1-2

31

HEARTFELT PRAISE

*I*n Psalm 138, David poured out his heart. There was nothing timid about David's worship. This is, after all, the David of 2 Samuel 6:16, who was "leaping and whirling before the LORD" when the ark of the covenant was returned to Jerusalem.

In today's psalm, singing before the King of kings, King David extolled God for His steadfast love, which compels Him to promise good things to His people. David also celebrated God's faithfulness, which ensures the fulfillment of every single promise He makes.

As David's life unfolded—from shepherd boy to warrior to the king, adulterer, and murderer who was still remembered as a man after God's own heart (Acts 13:22)—he encountered all kinds of distresses, yet again and again, the Lord enabled him to emerge unharmed.

In His loving-kindness, the Lord will also protect us. May we respond to that with praise from our whole heart!

Jacob said [to his long-estranged brother, Esau], "No, please, if I have now found favor in your sight, then receive my present from my hand. . . . Please, take my blessing that is brought to you, because God has dealt graciously with me, and because I have enough." So [Jacob] urged [Esau], and he took it.

GENESIS 33:10–11

32

BLESSED FORGIVENESS

Jacob and Esau were the twin sons of Isaac and Rebekah. After cheating his older brother out of the firstborn's birthright and their father's blessing, Jacob fled his homeland. When it was time to return, Jacob was afraid. What kind of welcome might he receive from his twin? Jacob needn't have worried. During the intervening years, Esau had moved on from the betrayal and was ready to reestablish a relationship with his brother.

Esau had needed to forgive Jacob. Whom do you need to forgive?

Jacob needed to ask God's forgiveness as well as Esau's. From whom do you need to ask forgiveness—and for what?

If we are in Jacob's position, let's confess our offense to the Lord, ask His forgiveness, and then go to the person we offended and ask for his or her forgiveness. Doing so may be pretty hard, but the Lord will be with us.

*I will bless the L*ORD *at all times;*
His praise shall continually
be in my mouth. . . .
*Oh, taste and see that the L*ORD *is good;*
Blessed is the man who trusts in Him! . . .
*Those who seek the L*ORD *shall*
not lack any good thing.

PSALM 34:1, 8, 10

33

MAKING PRAISE A HABIT

*I*n general, the word *habit* has a bad connotation: we too readily think of bad habits—like swearing or biting our fingernails—that we need to break. But habits such as saying, "Thank you" or drinking the minimum eight glasses of water a day can also be good.

What would it take to get into the good habit of praising the Lord "continually," not only when life is going well, but also when we're struggling? Maybe praise in those tougher times will be easier if we remember two things:

1. The Lord will always love us and want the best for us.
2. Life's level of difficulty doesn't mean God is angry at us or loves us less.

Life is hard, but hear God's promise: "Those who seek the LORD shall not lack any good thing." Let's praise the Lord for that truth—and keep praising Him as we go through the day, whatever it holds.

Thus says the LORD who made you
And formed you from the
womb, who will help you:
"Fear not, O Jacob My servant. . . .
I will pour water on him who is thirsty,
And floods on the dry ground;
I will pour My Spirit on your descendants,
And My blessing on your offspring."

ISAIAH 44:2–3

34

GOD'S PERSISTENT LOVE

*I*t is amazing that God continued to pour out His blessings on Israel, who too often fell into disbelief and idol worship. But even when they were unfaithful, He chose to blot out their transgressions and not remember their sins (Isaiah 43:25). Oh, Israel often faced harsh consequences for their sins, but God always welcomed them back.

It is equally amazing that God continues to pour out His blessings on you and me, who too often stray. But even when we are unfaithful, God chooses to blot out our transgressions and not remember our sins. He always welcomes us back.

And we New Testament believers know the blessed gospel: Jesus died on the cross for humanity's sin. We are blessed to name Jesus as our Savior, to know God as our Father, and to be indwelled by the Holy Spirit. We can show gratitude by talking to people around us who need to know this God who longs to bless those who don't yet know His Son.

Only those who are of faith are sons of Abraham. And the Scripture, foreseeing that God would justify the Gentiles by faith, preached the gospel to Abraham beforehand, saying, "In you all the nations shall be blessed." So then those who are of faith are blessed with believing Abraham. . . . Christ has redeemed us from the curse of the law . . . that the blessing of Abraham might come upon the Gentiles in Christ Jesus.

GALATIANS 3:7–9, 13–14

35

THE BLESSING OF ABRAHAM

*P*aul taught the Galatians that they should live by faith just as Abraham had. When God told Abraham to leave his homeland and go, Abraham did, because he believed that God would do what He said He would do. God accepted Abraham's faith as righteousness.

Similarly, we are declared righteous by our faith in God. Doing good works in hopes of gaining God's acceptance is not the path to righteousness. Instead, when we put our faith in Jesus—by accepting that Jesus is God's Son, who lived, died, and then defeated sin and death by rising again; confessing our sin; and receiving His forgiveness—God accepts our faith as righteousness.

Justification is the act of God by which He declares righteous every person who believes that Jesus paid the debt for their sin when He died on the cross in their place. Justification is God's act of crediting Jesus' righteousness to our empty accounts. Justification has nothing to do with our keeping the law. We are justified because we put our faith in the resurrected Jesus. That's why the gospel is such "good news."

God be merciful to us and bless us,
And cause His face to shine upon us . . .
That Your way may be known on earth,
Your salvation among all nations.

PSALM 67:1–2

36

WHY DOES GOD BLESS US?

Like the psalmist, we have undoubtedly asked the Lord to bless us. Often, we have prayed very specific requests, and sometimes we have made those requests for years. As wise believers have noted, God always answers . . . with "Yes," "No," or "Not yet." The fact that God answers our prayers is a blessing, but let's pause to consider why we ask and why God blesses.

We make requests of the God who created us and knows everything about us because He desires this kind of interaction with His children. As our heavenly Father, He wants us to go to Him with all our concerns and dreams, all our needs and desires.

In response, God blesses us because He loves us. As Jesus said, "Your Father who is in heaven [knows how to] give good things to those who ask Him!" (Matthew 7:11).

God also blesses us for His glory. Such blessings as peace, food, finances, or guidance reveal His glorious generosity, faithfulness, and love. So when people see God at work in our lives, may we give Him the glory by introducing them to our heavenly Father.

*Behold, I set before you today a blessing
and a curse: the blessing, if you obey the
commandments of the LORD your God
which I command you today; and the curse,
if you do not obey the commandments of
the LORD your God, but turn aside from
the way which I command you today, to go
after other gods which you have not known.*

MOSES IN DEUTERONOMY 11:26–28

37

YOUR CHOICE

When we read the Old Testament and see the sins of God's people and their refusal to change their ways, we are actually seeing our own behavior. Like Israel, we are guilty of turning away from God, wanting to be in charge of our life, and worshiping what the world values. We also face the same choice that the Israelites faced: Will we obey God or go our own way? Like God's people thousands of years ago, you and I are to choose between obedience and disobedience, between blessing and curse.

Throughout the Bible, God gives us instructions for how to live in a way that honors Jesus, our Lord and Savior. But will we obey? Will we align our thoughts, words, and deeds with God's commands and, as a result, know His blessings? Asked differently, will we be soldiers for the Lord, or will we live for ourselves? Will we live as if we don't even know Jesus?

The choice to obey or disobey God's Word is up to every individual. We know what God—who is waiting with open arms—wants us to choose.

He who dwells in the secret
place of the Most High
Shall abide under the shadow
of the Almighty.
I will say of the LORD, "He is
my refuge and my fortress;
My God, in Him I will trust."

PSALM 91:1–2

38

ABIDING IN GOD'S PRESENCE

As followers of Jesus—as people who have placed our trust in the Lord—we "abide under the shadow of the Almighty." We find in Him all the security we could ever want and will ever need. Confident that God will keep us safe, we experience rest, peace, and freedom from worry.

So what challenges does our day hold? Or—perhaps more relevant—what burdens of worry are each one of us carrying? We may be worried about work, our marriage, our children, family relationships, conflict with neighbors, or any number of matters.

The powerful words of Psalm 91, however, remind us that when we place our trust in the Most High God, He will be our Fortress. When we place our lives in Jesus' hands, He will be our Good Shepherd.

After all, the Lord Jesus loves us more than He loved life itself.

A day in Your courts is better
than a thousand.
I would rather be a doorkeeper
in the house of my God
Than dwell in the tents of wickedness.
For the LORD God is a sun and shield;
The LORD will give grace and glory;
No good thing will He withhold
From those who walk uprightly.
O LORD of hosts,
Blessed is the man who trusts in You!

PSALM 84:10–12

39

Turn Up the Passion!

*D*id you hear the psalmist's passion for the Lord, for worship, and even for the place of worship?

Does the average believer today feel this kind of burning desire for the Lord? Or have we become lukewarm at best, inoculated against such heartfelt passion by the dozen different Bible translations we have in our home or by our 24/7 access to worship music?

Or perhaps we live in a Christian bubble, rarely interacting with nonbelievers in any significant way. Or we may be so involved in serving at church—of course we're there all morning on Sundays, and we're attending Bible study on Tuesday mornings, working with the high school group on Wednesday nights, and mentoring a younger believer for an hour each Saturday afternoon—that going to church is part of the drill rather than a highlight of the week anticipated with joy.

May God use the psalmist's example to ignite or renew in us a fiery passion for worship and for going to His house. After all, worship is one blessing that comes to those who trust in Him!

Be doers of the word, and not hearers
only, deceiving yourselves.

JAMES 1:22

40

Doing, Not Just Hearing

We live in a culture that tends to consider people spiritual if they have an interest in spiritual things—a broad category that includes finding inner peace, determining one's purpose in this vast universe, exploring possible answers to life's big questions, becoming passionate about a cause, or getting involved with horoscopes, fortune-telling, or tarot cards. According to the Bible, none of this is actually spiritual.

Instead, the Bible teaches that those of us who hear God's Word *and obey it* are spiritual. God has given us His Word as a road map for life. When we choose to follow His map for us, we will find contentment. That journey, however, requires us to yield our desires to God and to live the way He commands—and sometimes that is extremely countercultural.

When we, however, choose to die to our own wishes and live with Jesus as our Lord, we will be doers of God's Word, loving and serving people just as Jesus did when He walked this earth.

Blessed is that man who makes
the LORD his trust. . . .
I delight to do Your will, O my God,
And Your law is within my heart.

PSALM 40:4, 8

41

DELIGHTING IN DOING GOD'S WILL

*A*s all of us realize, a simple-to-understand idea is not always easy to live out. And the description "simple, but not easy" definitely applies to our desire to trust the Lord. Of course, trusting God brings wonderful blessings like peace, hope, and confidence about the present and the future. Trusting God also means the blessed absence of fear, worry, and dread. We will trust God more completely and more easily the better we know Him.

We get to know God and His will when we read the Bible. Because He wants us to know Him better and live a life that glorifies Him, God gladly blesses our efforts to understand His Word. He helps us know His character with our heart as well as our head. In the pages of the Bible, He also shows us how He wants us to live so we're better able to determine His will for us.

Our growing trust in God and our greater awareness of His great love will enable us to join the psalmist in saying, "I delight to do Your will, O my God."

*Blessed be the L*ORD,
Who has not given us as prey to their teeth.
Our soul has escaped as a bird
from the snare of the fowlers;
The snare is broken, and we have escaped.
*Our help is in the name of the L*ORD,
Who made heaven and earth.

PSALM 124:6–8

42

HE HAS YOUR BACK!

ave you ever wondered about all that God has protected you from?

What would have made us its prey had He not intervened? What snares did God enable us to avoid? What escapes have we made as He guided our steps?

We may never know all the accidents we didn't experience because of our gracious God. We may never realize how often we were close to danger but continued on our way unharmed. But we may also be very aware of times when God did intervene. Maybe the car almost hit our car but didn't. Maybe the company where we wanted to work filed bankruptcy soon after that position was filled. In situations like those, we see God as our Shield.

The Lord protects us because He loves us with an everlasting love, and He is on our side. We can join David in saying this about our almighty God: "The LORD is my shepherd; I shall not want" (Psalm 23:1). We shall not lack provision or protection. Blessed be the Lord, our Helper and Protector!

Then [mothers] brought little children to [Jesus], that He might touch them; but the disciples rebuked those who brought them. But when Jesus saw it, He was greatly displeased and said to them, "Let the little children come to Me, and do not forbid them; for of such is the kingdom of God. Assuredly, I say to you, whoever does not receive the kingdom of God as a little child will by no means enter it." And He took them up in His arms, laid His hands on them, and blessed them.

MARK 10:13–16

43

JESUS AND THE CHILDREN

C learly Jesus was not too busy to welcome the children. Imagine seeing our child—or being one of the children—sitting on Jesus' lap, feeling secure in the strength of the carpenter's rough hands, and hearing His words of blessing. May we parents never be too busy to touch our children with the love of Jesus and words of blessing.

After all, our children are a gift from God, and we are to cherish them, introduce them to Jesus, and teach them how to live in a way that pleases Him. Today we have a lot of competition: social media and our culture at large loudly influence our children to do exactly opposite of what their heavenly Father wants for them.

Another lesson for us comes in Jesus' words: "Whoever does not receive the kingdom of God as a little child will by no means enter it." We are to follow Jesus with unquestioning faith, not worry about the future, be okay with not knowing and not understanding, and always be open to receiving His love. May we indeed have the faith of a child.

You [O Lord] meet [the king]
with the blessings of goodness;
You set a crown of pure gold upon his head.
He asked life from You, and
You gave it to him—
Length of days forever and ever.
[The king's] glory is great in Your salvation;
Honor and majesty You have
placed upon him.
For You have made him
most blessed forever;
You have made him exceedingly
glad with Your presence.

PSALM 21:3–6

44

BLESSINGS OF GOODNESS

*A*pparently speaking about himself in the third person, David was reflecting on the blessings the Lord has given him. Among those were God's call to rule His people, Israel, and God's preservation of David's life, both during battle and when Saul was in pursuit of him. We also see David's acknowledgment that only by God's hand did he have the glory, honor, and majesty of the crown.

If you have named Jesus as Savior and Lord, you have been adopted into God's family. You are a child of the King, and the Lord longs to bless you with His goodness just as He blessed King David. He invites us to ask for His blessings, but even all the blessings He gives us will never make us happy.

The only blessing that satisfies the human soul is God's presence in our life. Our deepest delights are found in Him, not in any of His gifts. So spend time with the Lord, meditate on His Word, and listen for His voice. Let God bless you with His presence.

Blessed are the undefiled in the way,
Who walk in the law of the LORD!
Blessed are those who keep His testimonies,
Who seek Him with the whole heart!
They also do no iniquity;
They walk in His ways.

PSALM 119:1-3

45

WALKING IN THE LAW OF THE LORD

*W*ho can disagree with the psalmist? Of course people who fully obey God's law and who seek after Him with all their heart will be blessed! But what about us mere mortals who are only able to avoid sinning when we're asleep?

Consider the purpose of God's law: "By the law is the knowledge of sin. . . . I [Paul] would not have known sin except through the law. For I would not have known covetousness unless the law had said, 'You shall not covet'" (Romans 3:20; 7:7). God's law reveals His standards so we can see how far short of His holiness we fall—and how much we need a Savior.

God commands us to "walk in the law of the LORD," yet He knows we will fail. That's why He sent His sinless Son. When we believe that Jesus died on the cross because of our sin, we are saved from the eternal consequences of failing to keep the law (Ephesians 2:8). Even so, we honor God by trying to live up to His standards, relying on His Spirit to help us.

I will meditate on Your precepts,
And contemplate Your ways.
I will delight myself in Your statutes;
I will not forget Your word.

PSALM 119:15–16

46

HIDING GOD'S WORD
IN OUR HEARTS

*M*editating on the precepts we read in God's Word
and contemplating the truth we learn in its pages
are activities that bring us pretty close to actually memorizing Scripture. In Hebrews 4:12, the writer made a
strong case for memorizing Scripture. God's Word,
he said, is "living and powerful," always relevant and
completely able to transform our hearts and minds. Its
truth is piercing, revealing to us our sin, our unkind
thoughts, and our judgmental attitudes.

When we lock portions of God's Word away in our
minds, those words can strengthen us in tough times,
enable us to love the hard-to-love, help us discern God's
will, and keep us walking along His narrow way.

Psalm 119:11 says, "Your word I have hidden in my
heart, that I might not sin against You." Hiding God's
life-giving Word in our heart and mind helps us stay connected to our heavenly Father in whatever circumstances
we find ourselves. And what a blessing that connection is!

Teach me, O Lᴏʀᴅ, the way
of Your statutes,
And I shall keep it to the end.
Give me understanding, and
I shall keep Your law;
Indeed, I shall observe it
with my whole heart.
Make me walk in the path of
Your commandments,
For I delight in it.

PSALM 119:33–35

47

TEACH ME, O LORD!

*I*t makes sense that the One who wrote the how-to manual for life would be the most competent and effective Teacher of those how-tos. No wonder the psalmist asked the Lord to "teach me."

The Bible definitely is, in a sense, a how-to manual for living in a way that honors and glorifies God. This way of living can attract others to the God who blesses us with His love, His peace, and His wisdom. The words of Scripture—the God-breathed words God has for His people—are true, and they offer us wisdom and understanding for whatever situation we face.

Furthermore, living for Jesus in this fallen world, populated by us sinners, is a challenge we cannot meet on our own. With all of its pleasures, the world calls us to live for ourselves and to pursue our fleshly desires. We can live for Jesus and for Him alone only if we are committed to letting Him guide our lives. So let's join the psalmist in asking Jesus to teach us how to glorify Him in all we say and all we do.

*Let Your mercies come also
to me, O LORD—
Your salvation according to Your word.
So shall I have an answer for
him who reproaches me,
For I trust in Your word.*

PSALM 119:41–42

48

TRUSTING GOD'S WORD

*O*ur faith in God may waver a bit when we face a huge loss or disappointment. Tragedy can make us wonder about the Almighty's power and love. In those times, will we choose to trust God?

Trusting God—and trusting both the promises He makes in His Word and what we learn about Him in its pages—is key to a blessed relationship with Him. He made possible an intimate Father/child relationship when, in His ultimate act of mercy, He sent Jesus to die on the cross for our sins.

Today we are as dependent on God's mercy and compassion, on His provision for us and His protection of us, as when we were first saved. We trust in His promise to care for us day by day. Our faith in this very good God is rooted in His unfailing Word. We read again and again—and we experience in our own life—that the Lord is trustworthy.

We are blessed to be loved and cared for by a God whose mercies are new every morning and in whom our salvation is sure.

I am a companion of all who fear You,
And of those who keep Your precepts.
The earth, O Lord, is full of Your mercy;
Teach me Your statutes.

PSALM 119:63–64

49

COMPANIONS IN THE LORD

E arly on in his decades-long teaching and coaching career, a friend observed the principle of the lowest common denominator among his high school students. Rarely did kids making bad decisions turn their lives around as a result of hanging out with students making good decisions. All too often, the kids making bad decisions pulled good kids into their world.

In today's passage the psalmist said, "I am a companion of all who fear You." That means people he spent time with loved the Lord, obeyed Him, worshiped Him, prayed to Him, and served Him. These people as well as the psalmist—like you and me—realized what an incomparable treasure we have in the Lord, and that truth makes us want to keep His Word. That truth also makes us want to know Him better.

The psalmist realized that he could know God better by learning more about His laws. That strategy is still effective today. We can also know God better by studying His Word. Let's invite our companions in the Lord to join us so we can be iron sharpening iron!

I know, O Lᴏʀᴅ, that Your
judgments are right,
And that in faithfulness You
have afflicted me.
Let, I pray, Your merciful
kindness be for my comfort,
According to Your word to Your servant.
Let Your tender mercies come
to me, that I may live;
For Your law is my delight.

PSALM 119:75–77

50

A HUMBLE HEART

Look again at the psalmist's words and listen for his humility. Although he was experiencing God's judgments and some unspecified afflictions, the psalmist didn't pridefully rage against God or arrogantly try to defend the actions that merited judgment. Instead, the psalmist humbled himself and prayed: he turned to God for kindness, comfort, and mercy.

Although the tone of these words is far from one of delight, the proclamation that "Your law is my delight" is proved true by the psalmist's turning to God during these hard times. Clearly he had come to know his God, and he trusted God's judgments.

Remember the New Testament invitation to "come boldly to the throne of grace, that we may obtain mercy and find grace to help in time of need" (Hebrews 4:16)? The psalmist was bold even as he was humble. Whatever the afflictions, the psalmist still approached God with confidence that He would help. God's tender mercies would be a fresh transfusion of life.

Oh, how I love Your law!
It is my meditation all the day. . . .
How sweet are Your words to my taste,
Sweeter than honey to my mouth!
Through Your precepts I get understanding;
Therefore I hate every false way.

PSALM 119:97, 103–104

51

MEDITATION AND
TRANSFORMATION

*A*s he often did, here David expressed his love for God's law and for God Himself. David didn't merely admire a passage from the Torah and then move on to the next section. May we follow his example. Let's stay with a passage long enough to meditate on God's truth. Perhaps we'll even choose to memorize a section.

Left to ourselves, we naturally lead a selfish, self serving life. We stray off God's path and away from Him. But to know God's Word is to know Him better. To know God's living and active Word is to experience His presence with us and to be transformed by Scripture's power. It is to have God's desires for us become our desires for us and, as a result, knowing more clearly His purpose for us. God's words can indeed be sweet!

So when we open God's Word ready to learn and obey, when we savor His presence with us, and when we choose to trust His faithfulness and love, we will experience the kind of peace and joy only He can give.

Your word is a lamp to my feet
And a light to my path.
PSALM 119:105

52

LIGHT FOR THE DARKNESS

It's both fact and cliché: we live in an upside-down and backward world.

In our Western, post-Christian era, foundational truths rooted in God's Word are no longer accepted or even respected. Living unmoored from biblical values and priorities, we are redefining marriage, deciding that more than two sexes exist, debating about when life begins so that we can end it, giving people permission to end their own lives . . . And the list goes on.

When we are left to ourselves to make a decision in this dark world void of God's truth, we may not always know which option leads to life and which one ends in death. We will remain in the dark until and unless we open God's Word. As the psalmist put this timeless truth, God's Word "is a lamp to my feet and a light to my path."

More specifically, we find in Scripture guidelines for living at the center of God's will. We find wisdom to help us make decisions. We find light to help us navigate this dark world, one step at a time.

Your testimonies are wonderful;
Therefore my soul keeps them.
The entrance of Your words gives light;
It gives understanding to the simple. . . .
Direct my steps by Your word,
And let no iniquity have
dominion over me. . . .
Make Your face shine upon Your servant,
And teach me Your statutes.

PSALM 119:129–130, 133, 135

53

THE WRITTEN WORD OF GOD

God's Word truly is life-giving, guiding us through the years on this earth and preparing us for eternity. Its divine message is timeless, relevant through the generations and across cultures. Its ancient wisdom speaks even to contemporary readers.

The Bible fuels our growth as believers. Its four biographies of Jesus—the Gospels—enable us to know Him better. This holy Book also paints real-life portraits of imperfect people who love God and whom God loves—and what an encouragement this is for us twenty-first-century imperfect people!

What a blessing that God not only gave us the Living Word—His Son—but He gave us His written Word as well. May we never take for granted the access we have to His truth set forth in Scripture, for His truth gives light and understanding.

May we show our appreciation of God's Word—and our love for its Author—by spending time each day reading our Bible, listening for God's voice, and responding with obedience.

I cry out with my whole heart;
Hear me, O L<small>ORD</small>! . . .
I rise before the dawning of the morning,
And cry for help;
I hope in Your word.

PSALM 119:145, 147

54

ONLY ONE SOURCE OF HOPE

*M*anmade systems of government and education, the economy, cultural norms, society's values, family members, a spouse, children, friends, neighbors—all of these can, at one time or another, steer us wrong or let us down. In other words, none of these—some of which are precious blessings—offer us solid hope for life. In fact, we can go only one place for the blessed gift of genuine, unshakable hope, and that place is the feet of Jesus. The truth and the hope we find in the pages of Scripture help us get there.

Imagine serving a God who offered no hope for either the present or the eternal future. Our God, however, is "the God of hope" who blesses us "with all joy and peace in believing." God also gives us the blessing of His Spirit who enables us to "abound in hope" (Romans 15:13).

Truly, the only real hope we have is in the God of the Bible.

Let my supplication come before You;
Deliver me according to Your word. . . .
Let Your hand become my help,
For I have chosen Your precepts.
I long for Your salvation, O LORD,
And Your law is my delight.
Let my soul live, and it shall praise You;
And let Your judgments help me.

PSALM 119:170, 173–175

55

CRYING OUT FOR HELP

*G*enerations after the psalmist composed this song, Jesus stated the simple fact that "in the world you will have tribulation" (John 16:33). Every human being knows the truth of those words: each of us knows some kind of pain, loss, and circumstances beyond our ability to remedy. But, sadly, not every human being knows the truth that, in all such situations, we can call out to the Lord for His help.

Clearly the psalmist knew to cry out to God. He knew well the God of Scripture who hears our prayers, who walks with us always, who can and does help His children, and who offers laws and judgments that teach, guide, and protect us. When we face difficulties, we can find wisdom and guidance in God's Word. Then, when—despite those difficulties—we choose to faithfully and unfalteringly obey the instructions we find in the Bible, we will know the blessing of God's pleasure with us. We can also be confident about His presence with us in whatever way His perfect will for us unfolds.

[Jesus] said to [His disciples], "But who do you say that I am?"

Simon Peter answered and said, "You are the Christ, the Son of the living God."

Jesus answered and said to him, "Blessed are you, Simon Bar-Jonah, for flesh and blood has not revealed this to you, but My Father who is in heaven. And I also say to you that you are Peter, and on this rock I will build My church." . . .

Then [Jesus] commanded His disciples that they should tell no one that He was Jesus the Christ.

MATTHEW 16:15–18, 20

56

SIMON, *PETRA*, PETER, ROCK

When you think of Peter, what words come to mind?
Maybe *impetuous*, *brash*, *outspoken*, *loud*, *self-confident*, and even *arrogant*.

So why did Jesus choose Peter to be the rock on which to build His church? Why did the Lord pick a big-talking man who didn't always come through? Jesus chose Peter for the same reason He chose Jacob the deceiver, Rahab the prostitute, David the adulterer, Paul the Christian-killer, and you and me with our failings and sin.

Jesus chooses unlikely human beings to play key roles in His kingdom, making it clear to onlookers that His power, not the individual's, is at work. Jesus also chooses unlikely us in order to grow us and transform us. By God's grace and because of His transformative power, Peter rose to the task Jesus assigned him.

Just as God grew Peter, God wants to grow us. Just as God used Peter, God wants to use us for His glory and transform us—make us more like Jesus—from the inside out. What a blessing to be chosen by God, used in His kingdom work, and made more like His Son!

Praise the Lord!
Praise, O servants of the Lord,
Praise the name of the Lord!
Blessed be the name of the Lord
From this time forth and forevermore!
From the rising of the sun to its going down
The Lord's name is to be praised.

PSALM 113:1–3

57

WHAT IF . . . ?

*A*ll that God commands or calls us to do is for our own good. Case in point, "praise the LORD" is sprinkled throughout the psalms (Psalms 7:17; 22:6; 33:2; 102:18; 104:35; and so on).

What good might result from our praising God regularly and sincerely? For starters, praising Him will keep our eyes on Him. When we're focused on God, we will find everything we need.

Now, what if praising the Lord were a built-in part of our everyday life? If we praised God as naturally as we breathe, what effect might that praise have on our attitude about life, on our perspective on the events in our private world and in the world at large, and on the strength of the hope with which we live?

Let's work on teaching ourselves to praise God not only when things are going well but also when things are going badly. Let's discover the blessings God undoubtedly has for us when we choose to praise Him in all of life's circumstances.

Thus says the Lord:
"As the new wine is found in the cluster,
And one says, 'Do not destroy it,
For a blessing is in it,'
So will I do for My servants' sake,
That I may not destroy them all.
I will bring forth descendants from Jacob."

ISAIAH 65:8–9

58

SHINING GOD'S LIGHT

*T*he Israelites were serving other gods rather than honoring the One who had made them His own, freed them from slavery under Pharaoh, led them out of Egypt, and gave them the promised land.

God may temporarily limit His unlimited love when we, His children, need to be awakened to the fact that we are straying from Him. In the circumstances of Isaiah 65, God said, "I will not keep silence, but will repay . . . your iniquities" (vv. 6–7). In an act of tough divine love, God withheld His blessings.

Maybe God is waiting to bless us too. Is He speaking to our hearts, calling us to live in ways that honor Him? Let's consider how well we're doing on that count: If Christ returned to earth today, what aspects of how we're living would please Him?

When the way we live honors God, He can use us more effectively as His light in this dark world. In fact, we may be the only manifestation of Jesus' love that our neighbors ever see, so may we let our light shine brightly!

Who may stand in [the Lord's] holy place?
He who has clean hands and a pure heart,
Who has not lifted up his soul to an idol,
Nor sworn deceitfully.
He shall receive blessing from the Lord,
And righteousness from the
God of his salvation.

PSALM 24:3–5

59

THE LORD'S THRONE OF GRACE

*P*salm 24 begins with the declaration that "the earth is the LORD'S" (v. 1), and that fact determines how we human beings are to respond to Him. After all—in contemporary jargon—He is God, and we're not. This statement of divine ownership makes indisputable the Lord's full right to reign over the earth—and over us.

And our sovereign God reigns in all His glory, power, and holiness. Who could possibly approach Him? The psalmist said, "He who has clean hands and a pure heart." The person who obeys God's commands does not turn to idols, lives with integrity, and has made a proper sin offering "may stand in [the LORD'S] holy place."

Jesus changed that. We are still to obey the command to love God and one another, we are to worship God and God alone, and we are to live with integrity. But Jesus, the perfect Lamb, willingly died, the ultimate sacrifice for humanity's sins. By doing so He opened the way for His followers to "come boldly to the throne of grace" (Hebrews 4:16).

The King of kings will always welcome us.

[The risen Jesus] led [His disciples] out as far as Bethany, and He lifted up His hands and blessed them. Now it came to pass, while He blessed them, that He was parted from them and carried up into heaven. And they worshiped Him, and returned to Jerusalem with great joy, and were continually in the temple praising and blessing God. Amen.

LUKE 24:50–53

60

GOD'S BLESSINGS, OUR PRAISE

*I*sn't it interesting that the last thing Jesus did before He returned to heaven was to bless His disciples?

And can you even begin to imagine how those disciples might have felt as they watched Jesus ascend into heaven? What a privilege to witness that!

Know that Jesus wants to bless us with glorious moments of intimacy and wonder just as He blessed His disciples. In fact, when we initially name Jesus our Savior and Lord—when we first sincerely and wholeheartedly surrender our lives to Him—Jesus blesses us not only with the gift of His Holy Spirit. Jesus also blesses us by adoption into the family of God.

And as God's children, we are to look to Jesus as our model for life. We will never lead the sinless life Jesus did, but we can follow His example and do our best to live in complete obedience to the Father. Jesus did only what the Father prompted Him to do. When we live that way, we will—as Jesus Himself did—glorify God in everything we do.

My refuge . . . is in God.
Trust in Him at all times, you people;
Pour out your heart before Him;
God is a refuge for us.

PSALM 62:7–8

61

A Refuge While We Wait

*W*hatever David was dealing with when he wrote this psalm—and whatever we're struggling with today—the psalm's truth is relevant: God wants to be a refuge for us.

When the storms of life are relational—a prodigal child, a rough patch in marriage—we can pour out our hearts to Jesus, our Savior, our Lord, and our faithful Best Friend. His 24/7 companionship can be a refuge as we wait for God's response to our prayers.

The storms of life may also swirl around career uncertainty or financial debt. Again, we can go to God who owns the cattle on a thousand hills; who knows our needs and will meet them; who provides food for the birds and who will provide for us.

More often than not, praying and waiting go hand in hand. When we look back at times we impatiently waited for the Lord's response, though, we often see that His answer came at just the right time. So, as we wait, may we take refuge in God and choose to remember that His timing is perfect.

I have set before you life and death, blessing and cursing; therefore choose life, that both you and your descendants may live; that you may love the LORD your God, that you may obey His voice, and that you may cling to Him, for He is your life and the length of your days; and that you may dwell in the land which the LORD swore to your fathers, to Abraham, Isaac, and Jacob, to give them.

MOSES IN DEUTERONOMY 30:19–20

62

CHOOSING OBEDIENCE

A flyover of Old Testament history reveals a pattern in the lives of God's people: they were faithful, they fell away, they missed out on God's blessing, they repented; they were faithful, they fell away, they repented. The falling away—the disobedience—often brought the curses Moses mentioned. The pattern is definitely predictable: obedience brings blessings, and rebellion brings judgment. Too often the Israelites, however, did not heed God's call to return to Him. They wanted to live their own lives and make their own decisions.

To one degree or another, we believers live like the Israelites did. We walk in obedience to God until one day we don't: we stray from God's path, we sin, we forfeit God's blessing, we repent, and we again walk in obedience—at least for a little while. Just as the Lord was patient and long-suffering with the Israelites, continually forgiving their sins and restoring them to favor in His sight, He will graciously bless us in the same way. May we not take for granted His amazing grace.

Blessed is he whose transgression is forgiven,
Whose sin is covered.
Blessed is the man to whom the
Lord does not impute iniquity,
And in whose spirit there is no deceit.

PSALM 32:1–2

63

THE JOY OF BEING FORGIVEN

*I*n Psalm 32, King David acknowledged the impact of his sinful involvement with Bathsheba. The prophet Nathan had approached David and told him a story about a rich man who, despite owning "exceedingly many flocks and herds," took from a poor man the only ewe lamb he owned (2 Samuel 12:2–4). When David expressed his anger toward that rich man, Nathan boldly told the king, "You are the man!" (v. 7). David was now face-to-face with his sin.

Before that moment, though, David's unconfessed sin had weighed him down. Day and night, David said to God, "Your hand was heavy upon me; my vitality was turned into the drought of summer" (Psalm 32:4). Unconfessed sin blocks our fellowship with the Lord.

The solution is simple, and it is a path to joy: "If we confess our sins, [God] is faithful and just to forgive us our sins and to cleanse us from all unrighteousness" (1 John 1:9). This promise is for you. Go to God and confess your sins today.

Know that the LORD, *He is God;*
It is He who has made us,
and not we ourselves;
We are His people and the
sheep of His pasture. . . .
For the LORD *is good;*
His mercy is everlasting,
And His truth endures to all generations.

PSALM 100:3, 5

64

BLESSED TO BELONG TO THE LORD

Let's look back at these lines from Psalm 100 and consider both the blessings listed and the blessings implied.

We are blessed that God is Lord of our lives. The almighty, all-knowing, all-good, and all-loving God will lead us more effectively than we ever could.

We are blessed that God created us. He is an engineer, a chemist, a physicist, and an artist all in one.

We are blessed to be sheep—clumsy, prone to wander, defenseless—in the pasture of the good and wise Shepherd who leads, provides for, and protects us.

We are blessed to serve and to be loved by a God who is good, who would never, for instance, demand self-harm or child sacrifice as a form of worship.

We are blessed to serve a God who is merciful. He does not and never will give us the punishment we deserve for our sin and our faithlessness.

Finally, we are blessed that our God's "truth endures to all generations." What a rock-solid foundation for life!

Great is the LORD, and greatly to be praised;
And His greatness is unsearchable. . . .
The LORD is gracious and
full of compassion,
Slow to anger and great in mercy.
The LORD is good to all,
And His tender mercies are
over all His works.

PSALM 145:3, 8–9

65

REFLECTING THE CHARACTER OF OUR GREAT GOD

*A*t the very beginning of this passage, we see that its theme is the greatness of the Lord. In His infinite greatness, God is truly worthy of our praise.

The Lord's greatness is evident in the unlimited reach of His generous grace and His constant compassion. We also see His greatness in the extent of His self-control and the limitlessness of His great mercy.

Many of us have been blessed to occasionally meet someone who unmistakably reflects God's grace and goodness. Whenever we cross paths with such a person, may that moment be a blessing of encouragement to us. May that person's example prompt us to live in such a way that we ourselves are clearly loving others with God's love, extending them grace, offering compassion, and being slow to get angry.

We can find no better way to live than to honor our heavenly Father by reflecting His character and loving people with His love. What a blessing to live in a way that not only honors God but also draws people to Him!

"Get out of your country . . .
To a land that I will show you.
I will make you a great nation;
I will bless you
And make your name great;
And you shall be a blessing.
I will bless those who bless you,
And I will curse him who curses you;
And in you all the families of
the earth shall be blessed."

GENESIS 12:1–3

66

Promised Blessings

God is a promise maker and a promise keeper. He will never break a promise He makes us. Whether or not we are faithful to His calling, whether or not we are obeying His commands, God keeps His promises. And in today's verses, God promised a lot.

The word *blessing* or *bless* appears in this passage five times—but only after God issued a command. When God told Abraham to leave his homeland, Abraham and his family departed for Canaan, the "land that [God] will show you." That initial act of obedience was a good beginning because, not having received a map, Abraham could at least cling to the truth that God blesses obedience.

And God had promised significant blessings to Abraham, blessings of land and of Abraham's descendants becoming a great nation that would bless the friends of Israel and "all the families of the earth." In fact, the God-given blessing that continues to bless families all over the world today is Jesus' death on the cross followed by His resurrection victory over sin and death.

Let the words of my mouth and
the meditation of my heart
Be acceptable in Your sight,
O Lᴏʀᴅ, my strength and my Redeemer.

PSALM 19:14

67

PEOPLE ARE WATCHING!

*I*t's been said that any one of us believers may be the only Bible some people read and the only Jesus some people see. As followers of Jesus, we need to be mindful of how we act and what we say. We don't want to give Jesus a bad name!

Through the years, Psalm 19:14 has helped many believers be mindful of the way we are living, walking, and talking. We want to show Jesus to others. If our words and the thoughts that generate those words as well as our actions are acceptable to the Lord, we're on the right track to being a decent advertisement for Jesus.

When our vocabulary is gentler and our actions are kinder than other people's, when our presence brings peace and joy, people around us will notice. When we are living with God as our strength and our Redeemer, we honor Him and, ideally, serve as a winsome model of life in Christ.

May the prayer of Psalm 19:14 help us consciously make the effort to reflect God more clearly in all we say and do. Watching people will notice.

When God made a promise to Abraham, because He could swear by no one greater, He swore by Himself, saying, "Surely blessing I will bless you, and multiplying I will multiply you."

HEBREWS 6:13–14

68

MAKING TIME TO
SAY THANK YOU

God wants to bless us with His love, mercy, and grace, and He does so daily in a variety of ways. He greets us each morning with the beauty of this world. He lovingly guides us and provides for us as the day unfolds. He mercifully forgives our sins and gives us fresh starts. And who knows what He protects us from? All this—and so much more—is grace.

Let's take a few minutes right now to consider the many ways God has blessed us. Do you have a job, clothes, food, and a place to live? Are you in good health? Do you have family and friends who love you? And you did nothing to earn any of this goodness, did you? More grace.

Why not begin a habit of stopping for a few minutes each day and thanking God for the everyday blessings that He so graciously gives you? Praise Him for who He is! Express your heartfelt gratitude for all He has done and continues to do for you. Thank Him for His faithful and everlasting love.

As for me, I will call upon God,
*And the L*ORD *shall save me.*
Evening and morning and at noon
I will pray, and cry aloud,
And He shall hear my voice.

PSALM 55:16–17

69

GOD HEARS!

*M*ost followers of Jesus have gone through at least one season of life when they wonder if God is even hearing their prayers. The best antidote to this discouragement is to look at God's promises. The unchanging truth in Scripture always trumps our fickle feelings.

For hope and encouragement we can, for instance, turn to David's statement of truth in Psalm 55. We read his confident proclamation that whenever he chose to pray and cry out, "[God] shall hear my voice."

The prophet Jeremiah echoed that glorious truth: "You will call upon Me and go and pray to Me, and I will listen to you. And you will seek Me and find Me, when you search for Me with all your heart" (Jeremiah 29:12–13).

Our Lord loves us. Our thoughts and our needs are important to Him. So may we never hesitate to tell God about our innermost desires and to share our heartfelt requests even when all we seem able to rally is a mustard seed of faith (Matthew 17:20). The way God works, that's faith enough.

Be of one mind, having compassion for one another; love as brothers, be tenderhearted, be courteous; not returning evil for evil or reviling for reviling, but on the contrary blessing, knowing that you were called to this, that you may inherit a blessing.

1 PETER 3:8–9

70

CALLED TO A HIGHER STANDARD

*H*ave you ever blessed with your words or actions a person who mistreated you? Have you ever seriously even considered that option?

God's commands to those of us who call ourselves Christians are very clear. We are, for instance, to love the Lord, love each other, and love our enemies. We are called not to harm people, but to do them good even when they have done us wrong. We are called not to curse people, but to bless them despite their acts of evil against us.

God blesses our obedience to these commands found in today's passage. One reason He does so is, when we choose to bless people—even those who have hurt us—with kindness, we are showing them the love Jesus has for them. Furthermore, our consistent choice not to return evil for evil will come to shape the way we think, speak, and act. God calls His people to share His love with the people around us who need to be loved—and that's everyone.

May we love lavishly just as Jesus loves us.

You, O God, have tested us;
You have refined us as silver is refined.
You brought us into the net;
You laid affliction on our backs.
You have caused men to
ride over our heads;
We went through fire and through water;
But You brought us out to rich fulfillment.

PSALM 66:10–12

71

BECAUSE HE LOVES US

When life is hard, God can seem silent or far away, but His apparent distance can actually be because He loves us. Our heavenly Father knows that a stronger faith and more intimate relationship with Him can result from the storms and fires of life. In fact, those seasons of loss and heartache—when we feel "affliction on our backs"—can bring about a more vibrant faith in God.

Verses 10–12 allude to the history of God's people, the Israelites. They were imprisoned, enslaved by the Pharaoh, downtrodden by wretched men, and exposed to such dangers as famine and military enemies. But God did not allow them to be overcome. Instead, He brought them through the fires and blessed them.

Sometimes God allows His people to be tested just as a silversmith tests and refines his silver. Subjecting the valuable metal to intense heat, the craftsman knows it is pure when he sees his reflection in the shiny liquid. God wants the best for us, so He tests and refines us until He sees His image more clearly in us.

"Blessed is the man who trusts in the LORD,
And whose hope is the LORD.
For he shall be like a tree
planted by the waters,
Which spreads out its roots by the river,
And will not fear when heat comes;
But its leaf will be green,
And will not be anxious in
the year of drought,
Nor will cease from yielding fruit."

JEREMIAH 17:7–8

72

WHOLEHEARTED TRUST

God created us so that He can enjoy our company and we can experience a dynamic and life-giving relationship with Him. It's a win-win situation, but when we don't invest in our relationship with the Lord, when we don't make it a priority, we lose out on many blessings and a lot of joy.

As the words from Jeremiah imply, our trust relationship with the Lord can be a source of hope, nourishment, protection, peace, and fruitfulness. We are also able to find strength from our relationship with Him, the kind of spiritual, emotional, and even physical strength we don't have on our own. When we lean on the Lord, whom we trust and go to for strength, we are better able to do the work He calls us to do with the excellence He deserves and the love He wants us to share.

It's an incredible blessing to walk through life hand in hand with Jesus. Don't miss out!

Blessed be the God and Father of our Lord Jesus Christ, who has blessed us with every spiritual blessing in the heavenly places in Christ, just as He chose us in Him before the foundation of the world, that we should be holy and without blame before Him in love.

EPHESIANS 1:3–4

73

SINFUL AND FORGIVEN, CHOSEN AND BLESSED

The people we meet in the Bible were human, and on occasion we read about their very human sinfulness. Consider David, for instance. This shepherd-turned-king-of-Israel, described as "a man after [God's] own heart" (Acts 13:22), committed adultery with the beautiful Bathsheba and then had her husband murdered. Yet still God loved David and blessed him.

We also read that Abraham lied about Sarah on two different occasions. Lacking the faith that God would protect him, Abraham told the leaders in the foreign land that Sarah was his sister. During Jesus' kangaroo-court trial, Peter denied knowing Him, yet later Jesus declared Peter was the rock on which He would build the church.

Time and again in Scripture, we see great men and women of God sin, but God always forgave them and even went on to bless them. Likewise, God will give you another chance and bless your life when you seek forgiveness for whatever you have done.

The righteous shall flourish like a palm tree,
He shall grow like a cedar in Lebanon. . . .
They shall still bear fruit in old age;
They shall be fresh and flourishing.

PSALM 92:12, 14

74

PALM TREES AND CEDARS

*U*pright. *Fruitful. Beautiful. Evergreen. Useful. Growing upward despite the weight of branches that can often be twenty feet long.*

When we look up the term *palm tree*, those are some of the adjectives and facts we find.

Stately. Long-branched. Durable. Strong. Grand. Can grow up to 120 feet tall. Symbol of power and longevity.

And when we look up *cedar of Lebanon*, that is what we learn. Having read both lists, we already understand more fully the images and the promise of Psalm 92:12.

God's righteous—those of us who have recognized both our sin and Jesus' death on the cross as payment for that sin; those of us who have accepted Jesus as our Savior—shall, by God's grace, "flourish like a palm tree" and "grow like a cedar in Lebanon."

So what *fruit* are we bearing? How is God *using* us in His kingdom work? Are we *growing* in our love of God despite life's burdens? Is our faith *durable* in the dark seasons? Are we relying on God's *power*?

Are we cooperating with the Gardener?

"You shall not make idols for yourselves;
neither a carved image nor a sacred
pillar shall you rear up for yourselves;
nor shall you set up an engraved stone
in your land, to bow down to it;
for I am the Lord your God.
You shall keep My Sabbaths and
reverence My sanctuary:
I am the Lord.
If you walk in My statutes and keep My
commandments, and perform them,
then I will give you rain in its season,
the land shall yield its produce, and the
trees of the field shall yield their fruit."

LEVITICUS 26:1–4

75

WALKING WITH GOD

As we start reading today's passage, we see that we're doing well on the obedience front, right?

Don't carve an image that you will then worship.√

Don't set up a pillar to honor some god you make up.√

Don't engrave a stone, set it up, and then bow down to it.√

But then comes a command: "Walk in My statutes and keep My commandments, and perform them." Suddenly we may not be so confident about how obedient we're being—or how obedient we're even able to be! We want blessings, but they seem contingent on our obedience.

Yet God's grace is a key factor. Yes, He extends commands and wants our obedience for our own good. But He knows we are made of dust: we fail; we sin; we mess up. In light of Jesus having already taken upon Himself the consequences of our sin, our holy God stands willing to forgive us, to maintain a relationship with us, and to bless us.

O Lord, *You are the portion of*
my inheritance and my cup;
You maintain my lot.
The lines have fallen to me
in pleasant places;
Yes, I have a good inheritance. . . .
You will show me the path of life;
In Your presence is fullness of joy;
At Your right hand are
pleasures forevermore.

PSALM 16:5–6, 11

76

THE INHERITANCE GOD HAS FOR YOU

What a comforting thing it is to be assured that we have a good inheritance, specifically a God-given spiritual inheritance.

This promised inheritance might have been especially significant to David, the youngest of Jesse's eight sons who would not receive any inheritance from his earthly father. From his heavenly Father, though, who loved him with an everlasting love, David would receive eternity with God as "the portion of my inheritance."

During his exile on the island of Patmos, the apostle John saw a revelation of our heavenly inheritance, of that place Jesus is preparing for us: "God will wipe away every tear from their eyes; there shall be no more death, nor sorrow, nor crying. There shall be no more pain" (Revelation 21:4).

May these truths about our eternal future enable us to live with joy in our hearts. What an amazing inheritance awaits!

Out of the same mouth proceed blessing and cursing. My brethren, these things ought not to be so. Does a spring send forth fresh water and bitter from the same opening? Can a fig tree, my brethren, bear olives, or a grapevine bear figs? Thus no spring yields both salt water and fresh.

JAMES 3:10–12

77

THE WATCHING WORLD

*T*hink before you speak."

How many of us have mastered that? Not only do youth and immaturity make us likely to say things we wish we hadn't, so does basic human nature. No one is perfect, and none of us is so wise that we always say the right words or do the right thing. Ideally, our remembering this truth about ourselves will keep us humble, dependent on the Holy Spirit, and yielded to His heart-transforming work in us.

Case in point: Early in my Christian life, I had a bad habit of taking the Lord's name in vain. Obviously I needed to change, so I asked the Lord to take that bad habit from me. Over time He answered my prayer; He changed what had been my default mode for years. Because of this heart-transforming work, I am free of that habit of taking the Lord's name in vain.

What we say—as well as what we do—matters. We are God's representatives in the world. What a blessing to have His Spirit transforming us so the watching world will see more clearly Christ in us.

Let all those rejoice who put
their trust in You;
Let them ever shout for joy,
because You defend them;
Let those also who love Your name
Be joyful in You.

PSALM 5:11

78

TRUST AND JOY

*L*ion and *Lamb. Lord* and *King. Love* and *joy. Trust* and *obey*. But *trust* and *joy*? This last pairing is not common, but David—the author of this psalm—linked them, and the linkage makes sense.

After all, when we put our trust in God, we do so not knowing what is ahead, what situations we will face, or what challenges we will encounter. But the difficult circumstances and the stress of the unknown matter less as long as we're focused on God, King of kings and Lord of lords.

Joy comes in as we look to God who provides for us, defends us, and loves us with an everlasting love despite our self-centeredness and sin. If this truth isn't a source of joy, what is?

When I was about forty, I realized I desperately needed God in my life, and I decided to live with Him as my Lord. That was the best decision I ever made, and today, forty-nine years later, I live with total peace because I completely trust the loving God to whom I belong—and I rejoice.

"Bring all the tithes into the storehouse,
That there may be food in My house,
And try Me now in this,"
Says the Lord *of hosts,*
"If I will not open for you the
windows of heaven
And pour out for you such blessing
That there will not be room
enough to receive it. . . .
And all nations will call you blessed,
For you will be a delightful land,"
Says the Lord *of hosts.*

MALACHI 3:10, 12

79

OPENING THE WINDOWS OF HEAVEN

When I give my address, I may refer to *my* home. When I talk about needing an oil change, I refer to *my* car. When I talk about who I celebrate Thanksgiving with, I refer to *my* children.

But who really owns our house and our car? And whose children are we taking care of? If we believe that all we have belongs to God—if we believe that all we have is on loan to us from God and that we are stewards assigned to take good care of what He entrusts to us—we are on the right track.

That said, according to Malachi 3:10, the Lord wants to open the heavens and pour into our lives more blessings than we can receive. We are to be grateful for God's generosity, willing to share whatever He provides us, and aware that our good stewardship honors Him.

The belief that our family, friends, and possessions actually belong to God stands in sharp contrast to the world's attitude. May our grateful way of living be intriguing so people clamor to know more.

Blessed be the Lord . . .
The God of our salvation! . . .
Our God is the God of salvation;
And to GOD the Lord belong
escapes from death.

PSALM 68:19–20

80

BLESSED SALVATION

*I*n Psalm 68—and elsewhere in his songs—David praised God for protecting him and his men in battle. He thanked almighty God for granting him victory, often over enemies greater in number and more advanced in weaponry. Such "escapes from death" were very literal for David; the word *salvation* had a practical life-or-death significance.

In the twenty-first century, God is still protecting soldiers on the battlefield; He is still preserving their lives. God is also still saving people from illness that could have been terminal. Yet here, on this side of the cross—when we know that Jesus died for our sins and rose from the grave, victorious over sin and death—we can see another layer of meaning in this psalm.

God is indeed the God of our spiritual salvation: He has saved us from an eternity of separation from Him (that's the very definition of hell). He has saved us from that eternal death. And He welcomes us into relationship with Him now and for eternity. So we therefore proclaim, "Blessed be the Lord . . . the God of our salvation!"

"This is the way you shall bless the children of Israel. Say to them: 'The Lord bless you and keep you; The Lord make His face shine upon you, And be gracious to you; The Lord lift up His countenance upon you, And give you peace.'"

NUMBERS 6:23–26

81

AN ANCIENT BLESSING

The priestly blessing in today's scripture has been used throughout history in synagogues and churches all around the world. These ancient words offer a beautiful closing when a time of worship ends. The words also provide a reassuring truth for worshipers to take out the door and back into the mission field of family, neighborhood, community, and workplace. Let's look briefly but more closely at the words that may be so familiar we don't really hear them.

To be specific, the Lord wants to bless us and keep us, to make His face to shine on us, to be gracious to us, and to give us peace. This God is the holy, almighty, eternal, and sovereign God of the universe and of all history—and He wants to bless *us*! This infinite God is at the same time our heavenly Father, and He wants to bless us. We're the ones for whom His own Son died. Read the blessing one more time, remembering that these are the words of God. May you hear them as being spoken directly to you, and may you know God's perfect *shalom* peace.

Blessed are the people who
know the joyful sound!
They walk, O LORD, in the light
of Your countenance.
In Your name they rejoice all day long.

PSALM 89:15–16

82

Have You Heard the Joyful Song?

So what is this "joyful sound" that blesses the people who hear it? The Amplified Bible, Classic Edition, says that knowing the joyful sound means understanding and appreciating "the spiritual blessings symbolized by the feasts," and the English Standard Version supports that reading with its "Blessed are the people who know the festal shout." We New Testament believers recognize that the fulfillment of the Passover feast was Jesus' death on the cross—the perfect, sinless Lamb of God bled and died . . . and rose again—and blessed are the people who know this joyful message!

We are blessed to know Jesus *today*. We know that one day "at the name of Jesus every knee should bow, of those in heaven, and of those on earth, and of those under the earth, and that every tongue should confess that Jesus Christ is Lord" (Philippians 2:10–11). But we already know Jesus as God's Son, the resurrected Victor over death, so may we celebrate that joyful truth by sharing it with others.

A faithful man will abound with blessings,
But he who hastens to be rich
will not go unpunished.

PROVERBS 28:20

83

WHAT KIND OF BLESSINGS?

What comes to mind when you think of "abound[ing] with blessings"? In our materialistic culture, we probably think immediately of stuff. Is that what this verse means? Is it at least part of what this verse means?

In light of today's pernicious name-it/claim-it theology, we must first state that we do not have power over God. We cannot, for instance, make Him act a certain way by obeying His commands. The Lord gives and the Lord takes away (Job 1:21) *because He is God.*

Our faithful God does provide His children with what they need—with food, clothing, shelter—and those are blessings indeed. A person who is faithful to God, however, will also experience the blessings that come from being in relationship with our loving, compassionate, and gracious God. Knowing Him and being known by Him, walking with Him, talking with Him, relying on His guidance, receiving insight into His Word—the blessings of being faithful to God are rich and varied.

Is your main priority in life "hasten[ing] to be rich" or being faithful to your faithful God?

Oh, how great is Your goodness,
Which You have laid up for
those who fear You,
Which You have prepared for
those who trust in You
In the presence of the sons of men!

PSALM 31:19

84

GOD'S GREAT GOODNESS

How can we begin to describe God's goodness? He loves us enough to let His Son take the death penalty for our sins. He goes before us, guiding and protecting us like a shepherd with his flock, and providing ways for us to serve Him by serving others.

When we consider that God is the Author of history and the Creator and Sustainer of the universe, we may marvel at His very personal love for us and at the blessings that, in His goodness, He tailors specifically for each of us. And when we recognize His Son as our Savior and Lord, for instance, He adopts us into His family. He also gives us His peace that passes understanding. He places us in a body of believers who will pray for us when, exhausted or discouraged, we struggle to pray.

We are truly blessed to be loved by the Good Shepherd Himself. As we follow His lead and receive the blessings of His good care, people may notice. May we be ready to tell them about our good God who wants to love and bless them as well.

"The King will say to those on His right hand, 'Come, you blessed of My Father, inherit the kingdom prepared for you from the foundation of the world: for I was hungry and you gave Me food; I was thirsty and you gave Me drink; I was a stranger and you took Me in; I was naked and you clothed Me; I was sick and you visited Me; I was in prison and you came to Me.'

"Then the righteous will answer Him, saying, 'Lord, when did we see You hungry and feed You, or thirsty and give You drink? When did we see You a stranger and take You in, or naked and clothe You? Or when did we see You sick, or in prison, and come to You?'"

MATTHEW 25:34–39

85

SERVING PEOPLE, SERVING JESUS

*J*esus often told stories to make His point—and to make His point more memorable. In today's passage His audience may have been surprised by where He landed. Rather than simply telling us to get busy helping the hungry, the sick, and the imprisoned, Jesus made that command more impactful by teaching us that when we feed the hungry, heal the sick, and visit the imprisoned, we are feeding, healing, and visiting Him.

Jesus' story both underscores the responsibility we, His people, have and motivates us to act. When was the last time we went out of our way to do something nice for someone? When was the last time we stepped out of our comfort zone to serve the hungry, the sick, or the imprisoned stranger?

Consider serving at a local food bank. Do some after-school tutoring at an inner-city school. Drive the elderly to church. Go on a short-term mission trip. Support financially a long-term missionary. Doing these things is doing the work of Christ, and—as Jesus said—doing this work *to Him*. What a blessed truth!

Sing praise to the Lord, you saints of His,
And give thanks at the remembrance
of His holy name.
For His anger is but for a moment,
His favor is for life;
Weeping may endure for a night,
But joy comes in the morning.

PSALM 30:4–5

MORNING JOY WILL COME

*I*t's significant that David opened this psalm with thanks to God. The Lord gave David victory over his enemies, blessed him with needed healing, and protected his life. With those details in mind, look again at what David wrote in the verses above.

Praise may not have been on David's lips during the battle, the disease, or the life-threatening circumstances. But David can indeed praise God now for His deliverance and grace. We need to remember what God has done in our lives, especially when, in dark, difficult times, He seems far away and deaf to our prayers.

May we be grateful for the ability to remember God's goodness—and grateful for His willingness to be involved in our life. Both facts about God enable us to believe what David proclaimed: "Weeping may endure for a night, but joy comes in the morning." God wants us to trust Him in the hard times, to know joy as we remember His hand in our life in the past, and to be confident that we will experience renewed joy when morning comes.

*Blessed be the God and Father of our
Lord Jesus Christ, who according to His
abundant mercy has begotten us again
to a living hope through the resurrection
of Jesus Christ from the dead.*

1 PETER 1:3

87

LIVING HOPE

*H*ear this truth as straightforward, not irreverent: *because we do not have a dead Savior, we have a living hope.*

Our living hope is rooted in the death of our Savior: Jesus willingly suffered the death penalty for our sins. But His lifeless body, hanging on the cross, was not the end of the story. Jesus' resurrection three days later meant prophecy fulfilled, sin defeated, and a living hope for what awaits us in eternity. And what awaits is "an inheritance incorruptible and undefiled and that does not fade away, reserved in heaven for you" (1 Peter 1:4).

The hope of God's ultimate victory over death, the hope that life in this world is not all there is, the hope that God will show us mercy and grace until we join Him in heaven—this hope keeps us going in the darkest of times.

Whenever God allows us to face seemingly hopeless circumstances to test, refine, and grow our faith, may we seek more fervently both God Himself and the living hope He offers for now and for eternity.

One thing I have desired of the Lord,
That will I seek:
That I may dwell in the house of the Lord
All the days of my life,
To behold the beauty of the Lord,
And to inquire in His temple.

PSALM 27:4

Choosing the Best over the Good

What is the one thing we desire most from life? Is it gaining status among our peers, or earning money, or being recognized for something we did? Maybe we long for a great marriage or a happy family. Or maybe what we most want is a life-giving, intimate relationship with the heavenly Father, who gave His Son so that we can be forgiven and spend eternity with Him.

If a relationship with God is of paramount importance to us, God will be pleased with that desire. He will be ready to bless our efforts to live that way.

But maybe our relationship with God is second or third—or lower—on our list, coming after some genuinely *good* things. Consider that order of priorities in light of the *best* thing—and the best is the fact that the Lord, who loves us with an everlasting love, truly desires to have an intimate relationship with us.

If we want—at least to some degree—to have that type of relationship with Him, it's our move. He's ready!

*The grace of God that brings salvation
has appeared to all men, teaching us
that, denying ungodliness and worldly
lusts, we should live soberly, righteously,
and godly in the present age, looking
for the blessed hope and glorious
appearing of our great God and Savior
Jesus Christ, who gave Himself for us.*

TITUS 2:11–14

89

Big Word; Simple Meaning

ere's our word for the day: *sanctification*. This million-dollar word simply means "the process of becoming more like Jesus." The Holy Spirit transforms our hearts so that, for instance, we sin less and love more. Hold that thought.

In His grace, God grants us salvation when we put our faith in His Son; we do not and cannot earn our salvation. Once we have been saved, we are to cooperate with the process of sanctification that God has designed and that—like salvation—we experience by grace through faith. Relying on the Holy Spirit within us, we are able to crucify our flesh so that we can please God by the way we live. We are to deny "ungodliness and worldly lusts" and lead sober, righteous, and Christlike lives.

To achieve this goal, let's work not on sinning less (a negative command that keeps us focused on ourselves) but on glorifying God more. Let's keep focused on God and His ways. He will enable us to love Him and love others—our purpose on this earth—and He will bless us along the way.

*I will love You, O L*ord*, my strength.*
*The L*ord *is my rock and my*
fortress and my deliverer;
My God, my strength, in whom I will trust;
My shield and the horn of my
salvation, my stronghold.
*I will call upon the L*ord*, who*
is worthy to be praised.

PSALM 18:1–3

9C

DEPENDING ON THE DIVINE

How dependent are you on the Lord? Do you turn to Him for wisdom? Do you seek His guidance? Do you trust Him with every aspect of your life and surrender all aspects of it to His care? What about when difficult, hard-to-manage situations arise? Then do you depend more on your own abilities and less on His complete knowledge of the circumstances and His total ability to handle anything you face?

An implicit invitation to choose dependent trust in the Lord, Psalm 18 describes the Lord as our Strength, our Rock, our Fortress, and our Deliverer. Why do we ever hesitate to put our trust in Him who alone is worthy of our praise!

This passage is filled with phrases that encourage us to trust in the Lord with all our hearts. So let's wisely fill our minds with the truth about who God is. The images in this psalm can help us hang on to those truths: God is, for instance, our Shield and our Stronghold.

God is our everything.

Trust in the Lᴏᴡᴅ *with all your heart,*
And lean not on your own understanding;
In all your ways acknowledge Him,
And He shall direct your paths.

PROVERBS 3:5–6

91

GOD'S WISDOM

*I*magine God saying to us, "Ask! What shall I give you?" (1 Kings 3:5).

When God asked King Solomon that question, he requested wisdom. Solomon had realized that only a fool tries to solve life's problems without God's help. In this life, difficulties, pain, and tests are varied but inevitable. Whatever you are facing, God wants you to go to Him for wisdom and in faith.

Look again at the opening line of today's passage: "Trust in the LORD with all your heart." Don't skip over that little word *all*. God doesn't want us to trust with just some of our heart; He wants us to trust Him with all our heart.

Thankfully, Jesus Himself reassures us that sometimes the trust we have can seem to us as tiny and insignificant as a mere mustard seed (Matthew 17:20). By God's grace, however, that amount counts. According to His promise, God will bless us with His guidance—for our good and His glory—when we place our trust in Him.

Bless the LORD, O house of Israel!
Bless the LORD, O house of Aaron!
Bless the LORD, O house of Levi!
You who fear the LORD, bless the LORD!
Blessed be the LORD out of Zion,
Who dwells in Jerusalem!
Praise the LORD!

PSALM 135:19–21

92

GOD IN OUR LIFE

*T*he Jewish people raised their voice in praise: "Bless the LORD!" Calling themselves and one another to join in the praise, they celebrated their God and glorified Him who had chosen them and delivered, protected, and provided for them. These words follow the proclamations that "our Lord is above all gods. . . . He destroyed the firstborn of Egypt. . . . He defeated many nations and slew mighty kings . . . and gave their land as a heritage . . . to Israel His people" (Psalm 135:5, 8, 10, 12).

We, too, can proclaim and celebrate the work God has done in our life. He is our God—our Deliverer, Protector, and Provider; the One who chose us to be in relationship with Him—and He isn't with us just for the big stuff. On any given day, He is with us. When we walk as He directs and do what He has for us to do, we experience such blessings as His companionship, fulfilling tasks, and opportunities to give Him glory.

We can find life a real adventure when we invite Jesus into our everyday life.

Gracious is the LORD, and righteous;
Yes, our God is merciful.
The LORD preserves the simple;
I was brought low, and He saved me.
Return to your rest, O my soul,
For the LORD has dealt
bountifully with you.

PSALM 116:5–7

93

GRACIOUS, RIGHTEOUS, AND MERCIFUL

*I*mplicit in God's very character is an abundance of blessings for the people He loves. After all, a loving God will love. A faithful God will be faithful. A powerful God will be strong. And—wonderfully—our God cannot violate His character. Furthermore, we read that Jesus "is the same yesterday, today, and forever" (Hebrews 13:8). We have the promised blessings of unchanging and eternal love, faithfulness, strength, and so much more.

In today's passage the psalmist both declared his love for the Lord and expressed his confidence that the Lord had heard his voice. The psalmist also proclaimed that the Lord is gracious, righteous, and merciful—and He can *only* be gracious, righteous, and merciful because such traits are the essence of His character. It is impossible for God to be what He's not; it is impossible for Him to be selfish, unjust, and merciless.

God's grace, righteousness, and mercy are unchanging aspects of who He is. Why wouldn't we welcome Him into our lives?

The Lord gave, and the
Lord has taken away;
Blessed be the name of the Lord.

JOB IN JOB 1:21

94

A BLESSING IN THE DARKNESS

The Lord had blessed Job abundantly, giving him seven sons, three daughters, seven thousand sheep, three thousand camels, five hundred yoke of oxen, five hundred female donkeys, and many servants. More important, this man "was blameless and upright, and one who feared God and shunned evil" (Job 1:1).

Despite Job's devotion to God, the Lord took away Job's children and all his material possessions. Yet his words in today's verse, spoken after his devastating losses, reflect Job's humility and his choice to be faithful to the Lord.

Living a godly life and obeying God's commands do not guarantee a life free of adversity. God allows loss and pain in our lives sometimes for reasons unclear in the moment and sometimes with the sole purpose of drawing us back to Him.

God wants the best for us. Sometimes that means giving to us; sometimes that means taking away. In those darker days, may we, like Job, choose to believe that our Redeemer God is with us and say to Him, "Blessed be the name of the LORD."

Blessed be the Lord,
Because He has heard the voice
of my supplications!
The Lord is my strength and my shield;
My heart trusted in Him, and I am helped;
Therefore my heart greatly rejoices,
And with my song I will praise Him.

PSALM 28:6–7

95

ANSWERED PRAYER

When we think back over our journey through life, what answer to prayer is the most significant?

In responding to that question, we might consider how long we prayed, how many people prayed with us, the way God answered our prayer, and the timing of His answer. Whether we prayed for days or for decades, whether God responded according to His perfect time-table or our desires, and whether His answer was what we had hoped for or not at all what we expected but actually far better, God's answer to our prayer is definitely a cause for praise and gratitude.

In Psalm 28, David praised God and expressed his gratitude for God's response to his supplications. May we never take for granted that God is always paying attention to us and always hearing our prayers. Knowing that fact, we can ask God for strength and protection, we can place greater trust in Him, and we can share our heart.

What blessings God has for us! Our heavenly Father loves to give good gifts to His children. Let's be sure to thank Him when He does!

Worthy is the Lamb who was slain
To receive power and riches and wisdom,
And strength and honor and
glory and blessing!

REVELATION 5:12

96

THE BIG-PICTURE PERSPECTIVE

*J*esus clearly warned His followers, "If they persecuted Me, they will also persecute you" (John 15:20).

Christian persecution today comes in different ways and in varying degrees. In the United States, Christian business owners may face boycotts, lawsuits, and financial ruin when they stand strong for God's values. Christians in the entertainment industry may be blacklisted and forced into a different line of work. Yet persecution around the world is far more brutal. Jesus-followers are threatened, arrested, tortured, and even killed when they refuse to renounce their faith.

Our financial support of international organizations that help persecuted Christians can make a difference, and the power of prayer is immeasurable. May we faithfully pray for our brothers and sisters who are suffering for their faith, that they will keep their focus on the One for whom they suffer. May they find the faith to believe that their affliction "is working for [them] a far more exceeding and eternal weight of glory" (2 Corinthians 4:17).

God is our refuge and strength,
A very present help in trouble.
Therefore we will not fear,
Even though the earth be removed,
And though the mountains be
carried into the midst of the sea;
Though its waters roar and be troubled,
Though the mountains shake
with its swelling. Selah

PSALM 46:1–3

97

WHEN OUR WORLD TURNS UPSIDE DOWN

The psalmist painted a vivid picture that may bring to mind images of the aftermath of an earthquake, the violence of an exploding volcano, the powerful swirling winds of a tornado, or the torrential rain and destructive flooding brought on by a hurricane.

On some days we may experience metaphorical tremors, gale-force winds, and unstoppable flooding that prompt feelings of helplessness and fear. Life's circumstances—a medical diagnosis, a job loss, the death of a loved one, and so much more—can shake our world. What are we do to?

If we choose to put our hope in God, if we choose to keep our eyes and hearts focused on the One who is all-powerful and sovereign, we can experience His divine peace; we can remember His great faithfulness to us in big things and small; and we will remind ourselves that we have no need to fear. God offers Himself—His rest, hope, peace, and guidance—in the midst of life's storms.

Blessed be the God and Father of our Lord Jesus Christ, who has blessed us with every spiritual blessing in the heavenly places in Christ, just as He chose us in Him before the foundation of the world, that we should be holy and without blame before Him in love, having predestined us to adoption as sons by Jesus Christ to Himself, according to the good pleasure of His will, to the praise of the glory of His grace, by which He made us accepted in the Beloved.

EPHESIANS 1:3–6

98

ETERNAL BLESSINGS

*I*t's eighty-eight words, four verses, but a single sentence—that we'll look at in four pieces.

First, we praise God who has blessed His much-loved children "with every spiritual blessing" and is storing those blessings in heaven. We have those blessings only because of Jesus ("in Christ") whose death and resurrection form a bridge between sinful us and holy God.

Second, God chose us from "before the foundation of the world" to know Him as the one true God. Go to Him for forgiveness and cleansing, and be blessed to be in a love relationship with Him.

Next, God's choosing can be described as "predestin[ing] us to adoption as sons." He enabled our adoption when, out of love for us and "according to the good pleasure of His will," He sent Jesus to die on the cross.

Finally, let us praise God for His kindness and grace. He didn't have to rescue us from our sin, but He did because—again—He loves us. And nothing in this world can separate us from His love (Romans 8:38–39).

Unless the Lord builds the house,
They labor in vain who build it;
Unless the Lord guards the city,
The watchman stays awake in vain.
It is vain for you to rise up early,
To sit up late,
To eat the bread of sorrows;
For so He gives His beloved sleep.

PSALM 127:1–2

99

CONSTRUCTION SUPERVISOR AND GUARD

Today's scripture lays out the truth that unless we are living in God's will, He may choose not to bless our endeavors.

Unless we walk according to the Lord's instruction and with His blessing, we cannot have the spiritual protection we need.

So may we let God build our house. May we let Him, our sovereign and all-wise God, guard our city for our good and His glory.

You see, God wants to lead us as a shepherd leads his flock, and He wants us to partner with Him in His kingdom work. He blesses us with His constant presence so we can sleep peacefully at night, confident that He will protect us and provide for us. And He, our servant Lord, wants us to know the joy of serving Him.

Do you know what the Lord wants you to do for His glory today? Ask Him—and watch Him bless the house you are building in His name.

I will sing to the LORD as long as I live;
I will sing praise to my God
while I have my being.
May my meditation be sweet to Him;
I will be glad in the LORD. . . .
Bless the LORD, O my soul!
Praise the LORD!

PSALM 104:33–35

100

SING PRAISE TO THE LORD!

The psalmist's joy is unmistakable!

When we consider the reasons this Old Testament man of faith was praising his God, we realize they are reasons that can prompt our praise as well.

For starters, the Lord blesses us each day with His loving-kindness and faithful provision. He guides us and protects us. He gives us strength for whatever comes our way. He describes Himself as our Good Shepherd.

Even greater blessings come to those of us who live on this side of the cross. Our resurrected Lord Jesus gave Himself over to death, to the punishment for sins He had not committed, to separation from the Father that He had never experienced. The perfect sacrifice for our sins, Jesus died on the cross and rose on the third day, victorious over sin and death.

When we recognize this truth and name Jesus our Savior and Lord—when we choose to live in relationship with Him and to make Him the center of our life—we have reasons to praise Him today and forever. We will also find ourselves living with joy.

About the Author

Jack Countryman is the founder of JCountryman gift books, a division of Thomas Nelson, and is the recipient of the Evangelical Christian Publishers Association's Charlie Jordan Lifetime Achievement Award. Over the past 30 years, he has developed best-selling gift books such as *God's Promises® for Your Every Need*, *God's Promises® for Men*, *God's Promises® for Women*, *God Listens*, and *The Red Letter Words of Jesus*. Countryman's books have sold more than 20 million units. His graduation books alone have sold more than 1.6 million units.